CONDUCTING
APPLIED RESEARCH  IN EDUCATION

CONDUCTING
APPLIED RESEARCH IN EDUCATION

Dr. Bunnie L. Claxton ● Dr. Kurt Y. Michael

Kendall Hunt
publishing company

Cover image © Shutterstock, Inc.

Chapter 9 and Educational Report examples screenshotted throughout © Suzanna Brawn. Notebook spiral graphic © David Michael.

Headshot of Suzanna Brawn on page 120 © Candice Wright, graph on page 170 by Kurt Michael, eagle on page 198 © bluezace/Shutterstock.com.

Kendall Hunt
publishing company

www.kendallhunt.com
Send all inquiries to:
4050 Westmark Drive
Dubuque, IA 52004-1840

Copyright © 2020 by Kendall Hunt Publishing Company

ISBN 978-1-5249-9159-3

Published in the United States of America

About the Authors

© Lee Claxton

Dr. Bunnie L. Claxton, Ed.D. is an adjunct professor of Liberty University, Colorado Christian University, and Longwood University. She has 25 years of experience in the field of education, including public, private, homeschool, and higher education. She has developed multiple graduate level courses, chaired dissertations, served as a research methodologist, and currently serves as a subject matter expert for applied research at Liberty University. Her scholarly publications include a book she authored in 2018 called *Planning, Writing, and Implementing IEPs: A Christian Approach*; she has also served as a contributing author for two additional books. Dr. Claxton served as the Superintendent for Liberty University Online Academy, an online K-12 school with over 6,000 students.

© David Michael

Dr. Kurt Y. Michael, Ph.D. is a professor at Liberty University. His experience includes 17 years teaching in the public schools and 12 years in higher education. He currently serves as the Administrative Chair of Doctoral Programs & Research for the School of Education at Liberty University. Dr. Michael has developed and taught multiple graduate level research courses and chaired numerous dissertation committees. He remains current in the field of education by presenting at conferences and publishing articles in education journals.

Overview of Textbook Features

This book is designed to guide the novice researcher through the process of conducting applied research for the purpose of solving a problem of practice in an educational setting or improving practice. The end result is an educational report that contains the details of a specific issue or problem in education and suggests recommendations for improvement. Features of this book are designed to support the novice researcher and include an explanation of applied research in an educational setting, with details regarding how to identify a problem of practice, instructions on how to create research questions, and guidance on how to conduct a thorough review of the current literature. After conducting a thorough review of the literature, the researcher will learn how to conduct applied research by collecting and analyzing data, which is followed by the recommendations by the researcher on how to solve the problem of practice or improve education practices. Though educational research is a challenge to define, and educational reports vary greatly, this book was designed to merge the two processes together with as much accuracy and authenticity as possible while remaining loyal to both the integrity and rigor of the research process.

Chapter 1: Introduction to Applied Research guides the researcher in discovering key components needed to understand and conduct applied research in an educational setting. The deliverable, an educational report, is described in detail. The chapter addresses the transition from novice researcher to independent researcher and scholar.

Chapter 2: Writing Front Matter for an Educational Report describes how to write a formal executive summary for an educational report. The researcher will learn to write his or her credentials, background information, and connection to the proposed research as the investigator. The application of sound ethical practices, in the execution of independent research, is disclosed regarding participants, permissions, and practices.

Chapter 3: Writing the Introduction for an Educational Report introduces the methods needed to write the introduction to the educational report. Novice researchers learn how to identify a specific problem of practice for a specific organization and describe why and how the problem is significant and requires further investigation. The guidelines for determining and writing the purpose of the research and the central research question are also established in this chapter.

Chapter 4: Writing a Literature Review for an Educational Report teaches the researcher how to conduct a formal and systematic review of the current literature. Novice researchers learn about scholarly voice, which requires formal language and tone. The deliverable for this chapter is a well-written, thorough review of the current scholarly literature that demonstrates competence in the understanding and presentation of the current existing body of knowledge regarding the problem of practice.

Chapter 5: Interviews and Focus Groups instructs the learner regarding data collection and analysis for conducting interviews and focus groups. The researcher will learn to write interview questions that are grounded in, and supported by, scholarly literature. Ten steps will be disclosed to help researchers effectively conduct interviews to gather data relevant to solving a problem of practice. Additionally, analysis of interview and focus group data collected will be divulged. The findings of an educational report will also be discussed.

Chapter 6: Surveys presents the specific methodology required for writing an effective survey to collect relevant data. Survey scales are introduced, demographic questions are discussed, and the eight steps for conducting a survey are explained. The chapter ends with a discussion on how to write the procedures and findings sections for the educational report.

Chapter 7: Documents and Artifacts specifies the difference between documents and artifacts. Five steps to content analysis are explicated. The chapter ends with a description of the methods for writing the procedures and findings sections of the educational report.

Chapter 8: Writing the Recommendations for an Educational Report includes the formal recommendations (Solutions to the Problem), which are the conclusions drawn from the data collection and analysis strategies. The roles and responsibilities of the stakeholders are described, as are the resources needed to execute the recommendations. The researcher will learn to evaluate and report the implications. The deliverable, which is the educational report, is fully achieved at the conclusion of this chapter.

Chapter 9: Example Educational Report This book concludes with an example of a completed educational report. This example is included to provide information regarding each section of the educational report. Readers are able to read the example to more fully understand the scholarly expectation required for each section of the educational report.

Table of Contents

CHAPTER 1

Introduction to Applied Research

Chapter Outline

Introduction
Applied Research Defined
Reasons to Conduct Applied Research in Education
Conducting Applied Research
Conclusion

Objectives

By the end of this chapter, the reader will be able to:

- Define applied research
- Describe the purpose of applied research in an educational site
- Explain the contents of an educational report
- Explicate a multimethod approach to data collection
- Explain reasons to conduct applied research in education
- Write an applied research question to address a problem of practice or topic
- Differentiate between gatekeepers, stakeholders, and participants
- List the nine steps for conducting applied research
- Differentiate between feasibility, accessibility, and logistics

Key Terms

- Educational report
- Applied research
- Site-specific
- Multimethod
- Evidence-based solution
- Site
- Gatekeeper
- Stakeholder
- Feasibility
- Accessibility
- Participants

- Proposal
- Logistics

Introduction

Applied research is a method in which the researcher seeks to improve outcomes by offering practical solutions for a variety of problems, challenges, and shortcomings present in almost every educational setting. Applied research is practical in nature. Educators may use it to improve academic achievement, assessment outcomes, social skills, challenging behaviors, teaching skills, or a variety of other problems of practice. Applied research offers educators the opportunity to make improvements by solving a real-world educational problem of practice through practical research that involves participants who are most closely involved with, and knowledgeable about, the problem of practice or topic.

The purpose of applied research in education is to solve a real-world problem of practice or to make improvements based on a specific topic using data specific to the setting or site and stakeholders. The deliverable is usually in the form of an educational report. An **educational report** is a document that contains the details of a specific issue or problem in education and suggests recommendations for improvement. An educational report is composed using sound data collection and analysis strategies. These strategies include determining the cause of the problem, investigating prior and present solutions to the problem, searching literature related to the problem, collecting and analyzing data, and making recommendations to solve the problem or to make improvements. Problem solvers are needed to address issues in education that need improvement. Thus, the key to applied research is problem solving.

Applied research is somewhat difficult to define and there is not one well-defined system for conducting applied research. The integration of qualitative and quantitative approaches into applied research continues to be a topic of much debate among scholars, and this type of research may be referred to by a variety of terms including integrative, combined, blended, mixed methods, multimethod, multistrategy, etc. All of these approaches attempt to integrate both qualitative and quantitative data collection and analysis methodologies into the research process (Bickman & Rog, 2009). Therefore, defining applied research in terms of educational research must be clear and deliberate, to the greatest extent possible, for the resultant data to achieve the goals defined by the study. This book seeks to define applied research in education and is designed to help educators solve problems of practice or make educational improvements based on a series of steps that direct the researcher through the applied research process from commencement to culmination.

 Go to *www.khlearn.com* to watch a video introduction to applied research.

Applied Research Defined

Applied research, in terms of education, is defined as conducting research using a multimethod design that incorporates both qualitative and quantitative data collection and analysis strategies for the purpose of solving a problem of practice or making educational improvements. Applied research may be conducted to add to the existing body of academic literature rather than fill a gap in the existing literature. Oftentimes, applied research in an educational setting is not generalizable since the research is **site-specific**, meaning that the research is conducted for a specific school, school system, or school district. Though the research results may offer new information, the results may not be applicable to other sites; thus, applied research is most beneficial to the stakeholders and the site where the research is conducted.

Applied research in an educational setting is conducted using a multimethod approach. In simplest terms, a **multimethod** approach to data collection and analysis refers to collecting and analyzing both qualitative and quantitative data. There is a growing consensus among researchers that multimethod research is more critical than individual qualitative or quantitative research alone. According to Bickman and Rog (2009), employing a multiple method approach to research allows for the needed flexibility to elucidate more information than can be acquired utilizing an isolated qualitative or quantitative research approach. The combination of qualitative and quantitative data can provide richer insights and raise more interesting questions for future research than utilizing one method independently. Multimethods, sometimes called mixed-methods, research is:

> An approach to research in the social, behavioral, and health sciences in which the investigator gathers both quantitative (close-ended) and qualitative (open-ended) data, integrates the two, and then draws interpretations based on the combined strengths of both sets of data to understand research problems. (Creswell, 2015, p. 2)

For the applied research educational report, the researcher will utilize both qualitative and quantitative data collection methods to solve a real-world problem of practice or improve a current practice. The applied research method provides the flexibility of the qualitative and quantitative approaches and data collection methods while allowing the applied researcher to answer his or her research questions in the most effective manner by making adjustments that are dictated by the research situation rather than a specific required research methodology.

As is typical in all research, applied research is subject to criticism. Procedures, theories, and findings are always subject to alternative explanations. Science demands that all findings be examined. This is part of the learning process and why research, and the analysis of it, is important. The point of applied research is to collect and analyze data and to learn how to apply that data to try to solve a problem or improve practice. Certainly, all problems will not be solved; however, many improvements are sure to be made by utilizing applied research in an educational setting.

Reasons to Conduct Applied Research in Education

Applied research in education is conducted to seek improvements in an educational setting by offering practical solutions for a variety of problems, challenges, and shortcomings present in almost every educational environment. There are problems in education, and problem solvers are needed to conduct research by gathering and analyzing data to offer *evidence-based* solutions to those problems, challenges, and shortcomings. **Evidence-based solutions** require the researcher to collect and analyze data and to use that data to offer a solution to a problem or to improve practice based on the evidence.

Reasons for conducting applied research include:

- to further understand human behavior as a means of improving educational outcomes
- to further understand a problem of practice as a means of improving academic achievement or practices
- to further understand a problem to generate a solution to benefit specific stakeholders

Applied research seeks to address the following questions, all of which should be addressed via a thorough review of the current scholarly academic literature and data collection and analysis strategies:

How can the problem of <u>(identify the problem)</u> be solved?
- What is the cause of the problem?
- What are the prior solutions to the problem?
- How would the researcher solve the problem based on the literature review and data collection and analysis?

OR

How can <u>(practice or issue)</u> be improved?
- Why does the practice or issue need to be improved?
- What prior improvements have been implemented to improve the practice or issue?
- How would the researcher improve the practice or issue based on the literature review and data collection and analysis?

Go to *www.khlearn.com* to watch a video about reasons to conduct applied research.

Conducting Applied Research

Below are the steps typically followed when conducting the applied research process. Note that, in some instances, the process is cyclical and overlapping.

Step 1. Find a site: The first step in conducting applied research in an educational setting is to determine where you will conduct the research. The **site** (or setting) of the research is defined as the place where the problem of practice that needs to be solved, or the topic that needs to be improved, is located. Examples of a setting include an elementary school, middle school, high school, alternative school, college or university, online school, home school, etc. For applied research, the setting may be further narrowed down to a classroom, a special education department, a media center, a college and career center, or a home for home-schooled students. Many other locations may be appropriate for research in an educational setting.

Step 2. Define the problem: The next step in applied research is to identify the problem that needs to be solved or the practice that needs to be improved. Begin by setting up a meeting with the educational organization's or site's leadership and discuss their needs. The leadership will include gatekeepers, and, in some cases, the leadership may want to invite stakeholders to be part of the conversation. With the help of the organization's leadership, discuss any problems needing a solution or concerns that need improvement. This may require several meetings before the problem is defined. Narrow the discussion to a specific problem or topic of improvement. Being too broad or trying to solve multiple issues can lead to a confusing and incoherent educational report. Gatekeepers and stakeholders are defined below.

Gatekeepers: **Gatekeepers** are defined as those persons in authority who make decisions regarding whether or not a research study may or may not be conducted in a particular location with specific participants. For some situations, this may be the principal or head administrator; however, in many school systems, research requests must be made through the county or district office where a research committee or the superintendent may hold the authority to make the final decision regarding research study approvals. When you seek approval for your study, make sure that you are speaking to the appropriate person who has the final authority to make the decision regarding whether or not your research is permissible.

Stakeholders: A **stakeholder** is an individual who is either involved in the applied research study or one who may be affected by the results of the research. For example, if your central research question is "How can the problem of low-test scores on the mathematics portions of the Academic Achievement Test (AAT) be improved at Hampton High School in Columbus, Ohio?", then you need to include all of the participants as stakeholders; you will also include others who might be impacted by improved AAT scores, such as students, parents, counselors, administrators, county or district level leaders, and/or state education boards. This is not always easy, as it is not always obvious who may be impacted. You want to include all potential stakeholders without including those who are not likely to be impacted. Stakeholders are different from participants in that participants are directly involved in the data collection process and stakeholders may or may not directly participate in the study.

Step 3. Consider feasibility: After meeting with the organization's leadership, determine if the research is feasible. **Feasibility** is the likelihood of the research being accomplished in terms of the time, money, accessibility, participants, and expertise that are available to you. If, after meeting with the organization's leadership, you determine that the study is not feasible, then it would be wise not to proceed. Below are some items to consider when determining feasibility.

Accessibility: **Accessibility** is the availability of a location and participants to the researcher who desires to conduct applied research. When considering accessibility, the setting of an applied research study may be determined by the accessibility that the researcher has to the location and the participants. Just because the researcher is familiar with a problem of practice at a specific school, it does not mean that the gatekeeper(s) of that school will allow the research to be conducted. Many researchers will be educators or potential educators who seek to solve a problem in the school where they are employed. Oftentimes, this is an effective choice since the researcher would have familiarity with the problem. However, if the researcher is not employed in a school or does not have access to a school, this may present a challenge for securing a location. In the latter case, the researcher may talk to school administrators to determine if there is a problem that the administration would like to have researched, or the researcher may present ideas to the administrators. A researcher must have accessibility to a location to conduct the research.

Participants: **Participants** are those persons who specifically participate in the research study by providing data. Determining participants for your study is exceptionally important to the research process since the participants will provide information about how to solve the problem. The participants need to be the people who know the most about the problem and can offer insight regarding a solution to the problem. When considering participants, first try to determine if participants are accessible and if there are any ethical considerations, such as dealing with minors. Also, determine the number of participants available for you to collect data from. Note that determining participants for your study is exceptionally important to the research process since the participants will provide information about how to solve the problem. More detail regarding participant selection in located in a later chapter.

Time: When considering time, determine if the research can be conducted in a reasonable time frame. Since many applied research studies will be conducted in an educational setting, it is wise to consider school breaks, such as summer and traditional holidays, as most educators will not be available for research during those times. Summertime often represents a 2- to 3-month break in many school systems, and those months are potentially a time period when participants are not likely to be available. This can significantly delay the research. Holidays are other time frames to consider. Though you may be away from work during a holiday and have plenty of time to conduct interviews, most administrators and teachers will not agree to be interviewed during that time since they are on a break from work. For example, if high school students need to be interviewed for the research, but school is closed for the summer, then students may not be assessible until fall of the following school year. This may clearly delay your data collection and thus your study. For this reason, you should consider "time" before and during the research process.

Money: Research often costs money. Money should be considered in terms of supplies, special equipment (such as recording devices), travel expenses, photo copy expenses, participant incentives, etc. While considering the study, estimate the total cost, and make sure it fits into your budget.

Expertise: As a researcher, you may be limited in your expertise regarding a topic area. For example, if you are considering solving a problem on the topic of special education, without proper training and experience in special education, you may not understand the jargon used in the field. Thus, consider your expertise in dealing with highly technical issues, and make sure you have proper expertise on a topic before you select your topic and conduct the research.

Step 4. Write the proposal: After meeting with the organization's leadership, put together a research proposal, and present the proposal to the educational organization's leadership. The **proposal** is a document that is presented to the educational organization's leadership as a means of communicating the details of the proposed research to solve a problem or improve a practice. The proposal should be presented as a well-organized and concisely written document. As a minimum, the proposal should consist of information about you (the investigator), ethical considerations regarding how you will conduct the research, a profile of the organization being studied, an introduction to the problem, the significance of the problem, a purpose statement, the research question, a review of the literature related to the problem, participants involved in the study, and proposed procedures.

Step 5. Present the proposal: Present your proposal document to the organization's leadership, and consider including a formal presentation, such as a PowerPoint presentation, that addresses each portion of the proposal. Discuss the proposal with the leadership and make any necessary changes as determined during the meeting. End the presentation by securing formal permission to proceed with the research as outlined in the proposal. This formal permission must be in writing and signed by the person who has authority to grant the permission to conduct the research.

Step 6. Consider logistics: Before conducting the research, make prior arrangements with leadership at the site and address any logistics for carrying out the research. **Logistics** are the requirements that pertain to managing people, securing facilities, and obtaining supplies. Before conducting the research study, ensure that all logistical requirements are addressed. Logistics are best discussed in terms of when and where data will be collected, from whom data will be collected, how data will be collected, how data will be recorded, etc. For example, if you are planning to conduct face-to-face interviews, make sure that prior arrangements are made to include the location where you will conduct the interviews and if the location is an area that is comfortable and free from distractions. If you will be distributing surveys to faculty at a school, make sure you check with the school secretary about the location of teacher mailboxes and a location where participants can return the surveys.

Step 7. Collect data: Proceed with data collection methods as presented in the proposal.

Step 8. Write the final report: After the data collection is complete, it is time to analyze the data and put together a complete educational report that includes a recommended solution to the problem or improvement of the practice. Along with all previous portions of the proposal, the report will also include an executive summary that highlights the study, discussion of the findings, and recommendation based on evidence.

Step 9. Present the final report: The final step in the process is to meet with the leadership at the educational organization that commissioned the study and discuss your recommendations. Deliver the final completed report to the organization's leadership and conduct a formal presentation that addresses each portion of the educational report. Discuss the findings and recommendation with the leadership at the study site.

The above are the nine basic steps for conducting applied research in an educational setting. Each step is part of a cyclical and overlapping process. The process of applied research in an educational setting is designed to solve a problem of practice or improve a topic. You must first find a setting or site to conduct your proposed research. Then, you must define the problem of practice or topic. You must then consider whether or not your proposed research is feasible, and if so, you must write a proposal. Once your proposal is written, consider the logistics and then you must present the proposal to the gatekeepers. At the culmination of the presentation, you must secure permission to proceed with the research. At this point, begin the data collection and analysis procedures. Following data collection and analysis, you will write a final report and present that final report to the gatekeepers or stakeholders. These nine basic steps are designed to implement applied research methodologies into an educational setting.

 Go to *www.khlearn.com* to watch a video about conducting applied research in education.

Conclusion

Applied research in an educational setting is a method in which researchers seek to solve problems through practical research practices. The outcome of applied research should be sound recommendations derived from evidence collected during the data collection and analysis process. The deliverable is an educational report that includes a clearly defined research process including the procedures and recommendations for solving a problem in education. This book will lead the researcher through the applied research process in an educational setting from commencement to culmination.

Chapter Highlights

Applied research is a method in which the researcher seeks to improve outcomes by offering practical solutions for a variety of problems, challenges, and shortcomings present in almost any educational setting.

The purpose of applied research in education is to solve a real-world problem of practice or to make educational improvements using data specific to the setting and stakeholders.

An educational report is a document that contains the details of a specific issue or problem in education and suggests recommendations for improvement.

The key to applied research is problem solving and recommendations.

Applied research, in terms of education, is a process of conducting research using a multimethod design, incorporating both qualitative and quantitative data collection and analysis strategies, for the purpose of solving a problem of practice or making educational improvements.

Site-specific means that the research is conducted for a specific school, school system, or school district.

Applied research is most beneficial to the stakeholders and site where the research is conducted.

A multimethod approach to data collection and analysis refers to collecting and analyzing both qualitative and quantitative data.

For the applied research educational report, the researcher will utilize both qualitative and quantitate data collection methods to solve a real-world problem of practice or improve current practice.

Educational research is conducted to seek improvements in an educational setting by offering practical solutions for a variety of problems, challenges, and shortcomings present in almost every educational environment.

Evidence-based solutions require the researcher to collect and analyze data and use that data to offer a solution to a problem or to improve practice based on the evidence in the data.

Reasons for conducting applied research include:

- to further understand human behavior as a means of improving educational outcomes
- to further understand a problem of practice as a means of improving academic achievement or practices
- to further understand a problem to generate a solution to benefit specific stakeholders

Steps for conducting applied research include:

1. Find a setting
2. Define the problem
3. Consider feasibility
4. Write the proposal
5. Present the proposal
6. Consider logistics
7. Collect the data
8. Write the final report
9. Present the final report

The setting of the research is the place where the problem of practice that needs to be solved, or the topic that needs to be improved, is located.

Gatekeepers are those persons in authority who make decisions regarding whether or not a research study may or may not be conducted in a particular location with specific participants.

A stakeholder is an individual who is either involved in the applied research study or one who may be affected by the results of the research.

Feasibility is the likelihood of the research being accomplished in terms of time, money, accessibility, participants, and expertise available to you.

Accessibility is the availability of a location and participants to the researcher who desires to conduct applied research.

Participants are those persons who specifically participate in the research study by providing data.

The proposal is a document that is presented to the educational organization's leadership as a means of communicating the details of the proposed research to solve a problem of practice or improve a topic.

Logistics are the requirements that pertain to managing people, securing facilities, and obtaining supplies.

CHAPTER 2

Writing Front Matter for an Educational Report

Chapter Outline

Introduction
Outline of an Educational Report
Writing the Front Matter
Conclusion

Objectives

By the end of this chapter, the reader will be able to:

- Describe the contents of the front matter of an educational report
- Explain what should be included on the cover page of an educational report
- Explain the purpose of the Table of Contents
- Write an Executive Summary
- Prepare an About the Investigator section of an educational report
- Explain gatekeepers and give examples of gatekeepers
- Describe the process of obtaining permission to conduct research
- List ethical considerations related to conducting educational research

Key Terms

- Cover page
- Table of Contents
- Executive Summary
- About the Investigator
- Gatekeeper
- Ethical Considerations

Introduction

An educational report includes many sections that must be completed thoroughly and that must be written in a business-professional manner. This chapter begins with the blank outline for an educational report. The purpose of this book is to help the novice researcher to complete this entire outline as a means of solving a problem in an educational setting. The educational report begins with the front matter. The front matter includes the following sections: Cover Page, Table of Contents, Executive Summary, About the Investigator,

Permission to Conduct Research, and Ethical Considerations. The front matter is a critical part of the applied research process since it introduces the reader of the educational report to the research. A good first impression is essential for an effective educational report; thus, it is important to be deliberate in presenting the front matter of a report in a manner so that it has a professional appearance that makes a good first impression.

 Go to *www.khlearn.com* to watch a video about the big picture.

Outline of an Educational Report

TITLE
  Prepared for:
  Presented by:
  Date:
TABLE OF CONTENTS
EXECUTIVE SUMMARY
ABOUT THE INVESTIGATOR
PERMISSION TO CONDUCT THE RESEARCH
  Permission
  Ethical Considerations
INTRODUCTION
  Overview
  Organizational Profile
  Introduction to the Problem
  Significance of the Problem
  Purpose Statement
  Central Research Question
  Definitions
LITERATURE REVIEW
  Overview
  Narrative Review
  Summary
PROCEDURES
  Overview
  Interviews Procedures
  Interview Questions
  Survey Procedures
  Demographic Questions
  Survey Questions
  Documents Procedures
FINDINGS
  Overview
  Interview Findings
    Interview Descriptions of Participants
    Interview Results

Writing the Front Matter

The front matter for an educational report includes the following: Cover Page, Table of Contents, Executive Summary, About the Investigator, Permission to Conduct the Research, and Ethical Considerations. The first page of the educational report is the cover page.

Cover Page

The cover page or title page of an educational report offers a first impression of the study, which signifies that the presentation is extremely important. The title page for an educational report should have a professional format. It should not be whimsical or elementary looking, even if the topic of the study is elementary education. This is a professional report, and it is based on the latest research and data available about a specific problem. Again, this is a serious document, and it should be presented as a professional report.

See Cover Page example below:

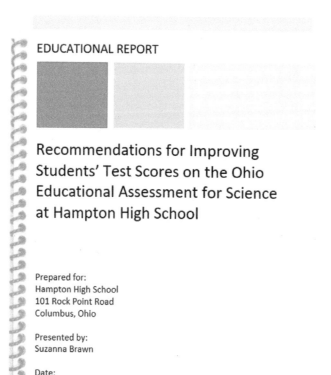

EDUCATIONAL REPORT

Recommendations for Improving Students' Test Scores on the Ohio Educational Assessment for Science at Hampton High School

Prepared for:
Hampton High School
101 Rock Point Road
Columbus, Ohio

Presented by:
Suzanna Brawn

Date:
August 1, 2020

Writing a Cover Page

The **Cover Page** of an educational report reveals the title of the study, the site, the investigator, and the date the applied research study was prepared or presented. The contents of the cover page should include a *title*, a *Prepared for* block, a *Presented by* block, and the *Date* the report was completed.

Title: The title should be written in all capital letters, and it should be derived from the central research question and the educational organization studied. The central research question should be converted from a question to a statement. For example, if the central research question was "How can the problem of students' low test scores on the Ohio Educational Assessment for Science be solved at Hampton High School?" then a possible title could be "Recommendations for Improving Students' Test Scores on the Ohio Educational Assessment for Science at Hampton High School."

Prepared for: The Prepared for section includes the name of the site where the research was conducted. Include the actual name of the site; do not use a pseudonym since this report is for a specific location and will not be shared with people outside of this setting. For example, this might be written as:

Hampton High School
101 Rock Point Road
Columbus, Ohio

Prepared by: This is simply the full name, including first and last name, of the researcher; a middle initial may be included, if desired. For example, this might be written as:

Suzanna Brawn

Date: Include the month, day, and year. For example, this should be written as:

August 1, 2020

Checklist for the Cover Page

☐ Does the cover page include a *Title* that is derived from the research question?
☐ Does the cover page include *Prepared for* information, including the site name and address?
☐ Does the cover page include the *Presented by* information, including the full name of the researcher?
☐ Does the cover page include the *Date* the report was completed or presented?

Table of Contents

The **Table of Contents** is a list, including page numbers, of the major sections of the educational report; it should be simple yet professional looking. The Table of Contents should contain one level of headings. It should appear in list format and not in outline format. The major headings should include the ones in the figure below, but these headings may vary slightly based on the specific applied research study.

See Table of Contents example below:

TABLE OF CONTENTS

Writing a Table of Contents

The first line of the Table of Contents should be the Executive Summary. The Executive Summary will disclose the focus of the study in a concise manner so that the reader may easily determine whether or not to read the full report. Following the Executive Summary should be the About the Investigator section that describes the person who conducted the research and made the recommendations. In most instances, this will include one investigator. Following the About the Investigator heading will be the Permission to Conduct Research, which details the permission obtained from the gatekeepers at the site where the research was conducted. An Introduction to the Study will follow, and this section will elaborate on the problem or topic of the study and introduce the next heading, which is the Literature Review. The Literature Review is followed by the Procedures, Findings, and Recommendations sections. The Table of Contents ends with the References and Appendix sections.

Checklist for Table of Contents

Does the Table of Contents include the following headings in this order?

☐ Executive Summary
☐ About the Investigator
☐ Permission to Conduct Research
☐ Introduction
☐ Literature Review
☐ Procedures
☐ Findings
☐ Recommendations
☐ References
☐ Appendix

Executive Summary

The **Executive Summary** is an overview of the research project and is the first section of the educational report that stakeholders will read. The Executive Summary will not be fully developed until the research has concluded and a recommendation (or recommendations) has been proposed since this information will not be known until that time (it is similar to an abstract in a dissertation or research article in a journal).

See Executive Summary example below:

EXECUTIVE SUMMARY

The problem for this study was that historically, approximately half of the students at Hampton High School failed to meet the state's level of satisfactory performance on the Ohio Educational Assessment (OEA) for Science (Ohio Department of Education [ODOE], n.d.). The purpose of this study was to provide recommendations to the leadership team at Hampton High School with possible solutions to the problem of students' low-test scores on the OEA for Science. Hampton High School is a mid-size suburban public high school in southeastern Ohio. The rationale for this study was that it is critical to implement efforts necessary to raise students' performance on the assessment since improving students' performance on this assessment may ultimately lead to increased funding and programming for the school, boost the community's confidence in the school, improve graduation rates, and prepare students for the future. For this reason, the central research question was, "How can the problem of low test scores on the Ohio Educational Assessment for Science be solved at Hampton High School?" Three forms of data were collected. The first data collection method was interviews with teachers and administrators at Hampton High School familiar with the science assessment. The second form of data collection was a survey administered to all science teachers at the school. The third form of data collection was documents from the ODOE. Data were analyzed and recommendations to solve the problem included establishing professional learning communities (PLCs) and providing professional development to teachers.

Writing an Executive Summary

The Executive Summary should include the problem, purpose, and rationale for the research. The Executive Summary should be approximately one page, as brevity makes the summary concise and more appealing to read. The first sentence of the executive summary is indented. The executive summary may include statistics and references; however, direct quotes should be avoided. The executive summary should be written using the following format:

The problem for this study was (state the problem). The purpose of this study was to (state the purpose). The rationale for the study was (state the rationale). The central research question was (state the central research question). The three forms of data collection were (state the three forms of data collection). Recommendations to solve the problem include (name the specific recommendations).

The Executive Summary should specifically state the problem that needs to be solved. This should be followed by the purpose of the study. Following the purpose of the study is the rationale, or reason, for conducting the research. The rationale should include one or two sentences stating why the problem needs to be solved. After the rationale is presented, the central research question should be included in the exact format in which it is given in the paper. Do not deviate when writing the central research question; it should remain constant throughout the entire paper. After the central research question is written, the three forms of data collection should be included. These will, in most cases, include both qualitative (interviews, focus group, etc.) and quantitative (survey, documents, etc.) forms of data collection. After the data collection methods, disclose the specific recommendations. All of the information in the Executive Summary section cannot be written until the culmination of the research project. At the beginning of the research, you do not know the outcome of the research (the recommendations). After the review of the literature and data collection and analysis, you will propose a recommended solution or solutions based on the information gained throughout the literature review and the data collection and analysis procedures for your study. Following the literature review and the research procedures, you will be able to fully develop the Executive Summary.

Checklist for the Executive Summary

☐ Does the Executive Summary include the problem of the study?
☐ Does the Executive Summary include the purpose of the research?
☐ Does the Executive Summary include the setting?
☐ Does the Executive Summary include the rationale for the study?
☐ Does the Executive Summary include the central research question?
☐ Does the Executive Summary include the procedures?
☐ Does the Executive Summary include the recommendations?
☐ The Executive Summary is approximately one page (no longer).
☐ The Executive Summary does not include quotes.
☐ The Executive Summary is in paragraph format.
☐ The Executive Summary is written in past tense.

About the Investigator

The **About the Investigator** section of the educational report should disclose information about the person who conducted the research. Limit the information in this section to professional information and credentials.

See About the Investigator example below:

ABOUT THE INVESTIGATOR

Suzanna Brawn is a science teacher at Hampton High School. She has been teaching in the Ohio public school system for twelve years. She earned a bachelor's degree from Town College and has a Master of Education degree from State University. She is currently pursuing an Ed.D. in education from West University with a cognate in science education. Suzanna was previously employed as an instructional coach for science teachers for a school district just outside of Columbus, Ohio. Her instructional coach experience provided her the opportunity to make suggestions to science teachers, science departments, and administrators regarding daily instruction, assessment, and data analysis. As a science teacher at Hampton High School, Suzanna is motivated to improve students test scores on the Ohio Educational Assessment (OEA) for Science. Because she is currently employed by the school within the school's science department, she recognizes that bias and assumptions may have been brought to this study. However, as a researcher, she believes that through a systematic research approach, bias was limited.

Headshot © Candice Wright

Writing the About the Investigator Section

The About the Investigator section should include the researcher's professional credentials. Include a professional headshot photograph. This photograph must be a business professional picture, and it should not be a picture with others evidently cropped out of the picture. A solid color background and complimentary solid colored clothing are preferred. The background of the portrait and the clothing choice should coordinate with the colors chosen for the Cover Page. For example, if green and orange are the colors chosen for the Cover Page, then colors that clash with green and orange (such as hot pink) should not be evident in the headshot.

The About the Investigator section should include a clear and thorough explanation of the researcher's relationship to the site and a statement about any bias or assumptions the researcher may bring to the project and that may influence data collection and analysis. All researchers have biases, so you must be forthright in your presentation of this information. This section should be approximately a half page long; it should not exceed one page.

Checklist for About the Investigator

☐ Does the About the Investigator section include the researcher's name?

☐ Does the About the Investigator section include the researcher's professional credentials?

☐ Does the About the Investigator section include a clear description of the researcher's relationship to the educational site?

☐ Does the About the Investigator section include biases?

☐ Does the About the Investigator section include a professional headshot portrait?

☐ The About the Investigator section is written in paragraph format.

☐ The About the Investigator section is written in present and/or past tense.

☐ The About the Investigator section is less than one page in length.

Permission to Conduct the Research

Permission must be sought from the appropriate person(s) prior to conducting any research. When you seek approval for your study, make sure that you are speaking to the appropriate person who has the final authority to make the decision regarding whether or not your proposed research is permissible. **Gatekeepers** are those persons in authority who make decisions regarding whether or not a research study may or may not be conducted in a particular location with specific participants. It is best to get permission in writing and on official letter head. The approval letter should be included as an appendix at the end of the educational report.

See Permission to Conduct the Research example below:

Permission

Permission was secured from the principal of Hampton High School to conduct the research at the school and to utilize information available regarding the school's performance on the Ohio Educational Assessment (OEA) for Science. See Appendix A for permission letter.

See Permission Letter example below:

APPENDIX A

August 16, 2019

Hampton High School
101 Rock Point Road
Columbus, Ohio

Dear Suzanna Brawn,

After careful review of your research proposal entitled, *Improving Students' Scores on the Ohio Educational Assessment for Science*, I have decided to grant you permission to conduct your research at Hampton High School in the Columbus, OH.

Sincerely,

Jenny Keller

Jenny J. Keller, Principal
(867) 555-5309

82 | Page

Eagle © bluezace/Shutterstock.com

Writing a Permission to Conduct the Research Section

The Permission to Conduct Research section includes written permission (preferably on school/company letterhead) from the gatekeeper(s) for the site of the proposed research. This letter should be attached as an appendix, and a narrative section must be written that describes who granted the permission to conduct the research. When seeking permission to conduct the research, it is important to seek it from the source, or gatekeeper, who actually has the authority to make that decision. Sometimes the administrator of a school, such as the principal, has the authority to allow research to be conducted, and sometimes permission must be sought from a higher level of authority, such as the superintendent or a specific research team at a district office. Rarely does a classroom teacher have the final authority to grant permission to conduct formal research in an educational setting. Permission to conduct the research should be sought early on in the process to ensure that you have a viable site where you can conduct the research.

Checklist for Permission to Conduct the Research

☐ Does the Permission to Conduct research section include the name of the gatekeeper(s) and their position (principal, superintendent, etc.)?

☐ Does the Permission to Conduct research section include a reference to the appendix where the written permission letter is located? (For example: See Appendix A).

☐ The Permission to Conduct the Research section is written in narrative paragraph format.

☐ The Permission to Conduct the Research section is written in past tense.

Ethical Considerations

Ethical considerations for applied educational research include all practices that involve the treatment of human subjects. In this portion of the report, discuss ethical considerations that need to be considered while conducting the research and the treatment of participants who are part of the research. All research needs to be conducted ethically, and ethical practices must be carefully considered when research involves human participants (Yin, 2014). People conducting applied research ultimately desire to influence the beliefs and behaviors of gatekeepers, stakeholders, and/or participants to improve a real-life problem or topic, in a real-life setting. Influencing the behaviors of the participants is typically not problematic since the ultimate goal of educational research is to make improvements by solving a problem or improving a practice, and because educational researchers seek to serve those who participate in their research by offering a solution to an existing problem. However, caution must be exercised throughout the research process to ensure that participants are treated ethically.

See Ethical Considerations example on the following page:

Ethical Considerations

Ethical practices for applied research should be beneficial and should include limited risk to participants; thus, the researcher ensured that, as compared to the benefits of the study, participants did not endure more than minimal risk. Participants were elicited via personal communication. Participants included science teachers and administrators at Hampton High School. Pseudonyms are used to protect the identity of the participants. Interviews were conducted off-campus, which provided an additional level of confidentiality for participants. Identifying information was not collected during the survey process. The documents were collected from a public website. All materials were stored electronically with password protection. These ethical considerations were incorporated into this study to preserve the integrity of the process and results of the study. The information contained in this report is intended to solve a specific problem at a specific location and is not generalizable to a broader population. Therefore, the information will not be shared or distributed outside of Hampton High School. For this reason, Institutional Review Board (IRB) approval was not required.

Writing an Ethical Considerations Section

The Ethical Considerations section should include information pertaining to the treatment of human subjects and how you will ensure ethical treatment while conducting your research. Participants in the study must have their identifying information protected. Data collected that could possibly be used to identify participants must be safeguarded. To protect data, you are encouraged to store all information you view and analyze via computer on a removable storage device (such as a thumb drive or similar device). When not in use, the computer (if data are stored on it) and any removable memory device should be stored in a locked cabinet or room to prevent anyone other than you, the researcher, from gaining access to the information.

According to Creswell and Poth (2018), data collection involves "anticipating ethical issues involved in gaining permissions, conducting a good sampling strategy, developing means for recording information, responding to issues as they arrive in the field, and storing the data securely" (p. 147). As a researcher, it is your responsibility to protect the identity of the school system, school, participants, business, and all people and places involved in the study. This protection includes the storage of data as well as conversations regarding the information.

In some situations, it may be wise to use pseudonyms. **Pseudonyms** are fictitious names that are used in place of real names to protect the identity of the participants and the setting. Possible pseudonym options include assigning typical pseudonym names or choosing bland pseudonym labels. *Typical pseudonym* names given to people and places should not be unique or extravagant names; rather, you should choose names that are typical for the population or location where you will conduct the research. Examples of possible typical pseudonym choices include: Prairie School District, Mountain High School, Southwest Middle School, Elizabeth, Taylor, Mary, Jade, Chris, Harley, Jordan, Darryl, Pat, Jack, Marquis, etc. Choose pseudonyms that reflect the culture of the school, business, and participants.

Bland pseudonym labels for people and places should follow logical position and/or location titles. Examples of possible bland pseudonym choices include: Administrator A, Administrator B, Teacher A, Teacher B, Teacher C, Elementary School A, Elementary School B, Elementary School C, High School X, High School Y, High School Z, etc. These pseudonyms are not reflective of the culture of the school or participants but are generic in presentation.

You should respect the privacy and anonymity of participants. Information that is disclosed by the participants should NEVER be reported in a manner that could link the participant to the information. If an administrator or teacher seeks information about a respondent after the results of a survey are disclosed, it is your ethical obligation NOT to disclose that information. For example, if survey results indicate that a teacher is absent due to a negative perception of leadership, the administration may seek to obtain the information regarding the identity of the participant from you; however, you are ethically obligated to decline to share that information.

In many cases of applied educational research using the template in this book, Institutional Review Board (IRB) approval will not be necessary. However, in some cases, IRB approval may be required. For example, if your study includes any degree of deception, IRB approval is required. If your study includes sensitive information, a protected class, or vulnerable populations, IRB approval may be required. Your research may be exempt from the requirement of IRB approval if it involves minimal or no risk to participants. You must check with your cooperating institution to determine whether or not IRB approval is required for your specific research. Also, when working with minor participants, you should always check with your project sites regarding whether parental permission will be needed before you survey or interview students who are minors.

Checklist for Ethical Considerations

☐ Does the Ethical Considerations section include a description of ethical treatment of participants specific to your study?

☐ Does the Ethical Considerations section include solicitation of participants procedures?

☐ Does the Ethical Considerations section include a brief description of the specific participants (teachers, administrators, etc.)?

☐ Does the Ethical Considerations section include data protection strategies (i.e., pseudonyms)?

☐ Does the Ethical Considerations section include storage of data strategies?

☐ Does the Ethical Considerations section include IRB permission, if applicable?

☐ The Ethical Considerations section is written in paragraph format.

☐ The Ethical Considerations section is written in past tense.

Conclusion

The front matter of an educational report is a lot of information in relatively few pages. The information needs to be written professionally and concisely to communicate as much as possible in as few words as are necessary. The front matter begins with a professionally presented Cover Page. The Cover Page is followed by a concise Table of Contents with one level of headings and only includes the major sections of the report. At the culmination of the study, the Executive Summary will be written to include a brief synopsis of the study with recommendations. The About the Investigator section will disclose information about the research of the study. This is followed by the Permissions to Conduct the study and Ethical Considerations. The front matter offers a first impression; thus, this is important information that must be presented professionally, effectively, and concisely.

Chapter Highlights

The educational report begins with the front matter. The front matter includes the Cover Page, Table of Contents, Executive Summary, About the Investigator, Permission to Conduct Research, and Ethical Considerations.

The Cover Page or title page for an applied research report offers a first impression of the study, which makes its presentation extremely important.

The Cover Page of an educational report reveals the title of the study, the site, the investigator, and the date the applied research study was prepared/presented.

The Table of Contents is a list, including page numbers, of the major sections of the educational report; it should be simple yet professional looking.

The Table of Contents should contain one level of headings. It should appear in list format and not in outline format.

The Executive Summary is an overview of the research project and is the first section of the educational report that stakeholders will read.

The Executive Summary should be completed after the research has been conducted.

The About the Investigator section of the educational report should disclose information about the person who conducted the research. The information in this section needs to include only professional information and credentials.

The About the Investigator section includes a professional headshot photograph of the investigator.

The Permission to Conduct Research section includes written permission from the gatekeepers of the site for the research.

Gatekeepers are those persons in authority who make decisions regarding whether or not a research study may or may not be conducted in a particular location and with specific participants.

Ethical considerations for applied educational research include all practices that involve the treatment of human subjects. All research needs to be conducted ethically, and ethics must be carefully considered when research involves human participants (Yin, 2014).

The Ethical Considerations should include information pertaining to the treatment of human subjects and how the research will ensure ethical treatment while conducting research.

Pseudonyms are fictitious names that are used in place of real names to protect the identity of the participants and the site. Possible pseudonym options include assigning typical pseudonym names or choosing bland pseudonym labels.

In many cases of applied educational research, Institutional Review Board (IRB) approval is not necessary. Cooperating institutions determine whether or not IRB approval is required for specific research.

CHAPTER 3

Writing the Introduction for an Educational Report

Objectives

By the end of this chapter, the reader will be able to:

- List the sections of the Introduction section of an educational report
- Write an Introduction for an applied research study
- Describe the contents of an Organizational Profile
- Explain what is meant by problem of practice
- Identify a problem of practice for an applied research topic
- Write a Significance of the Problem section for an applied research topic
- Write a Purpose Statement for an applied research study
- Write a Central Research Question for an applied research study
- Explain the importance of including definitions in an applied research manuscript

Key Terms

- Introduction to the study
- Organizational Profile
- Problem of practice
- Significance of the problem
- Purpose statement
- Central research question
- Definitions

Introduction

The Introduction to an educational report section presents the study in a concise manner, but it is not written as concisely as the executive summary. The **Introduction to the study** introduces the reader to the topic of the research and the problem to be solved. The Introduction includes the Organizational Profile, an Introduction to the Problem, the Significance of the Problem, the Purpose Statement, the Central Research Question, and the Definitions related to the research. The first section of the Introduction is the Organizational Profile.

 Go to *www.khlearn.com* to watch a video about choosing a problem of practice to research.

Overview

The Overview for each section of the educational report should include two major pieces of information: (1) the purpose of the study and (2) an introduction to the major headings that will be presented.
See Overview example below:

INTRODUCTION

Overview

The purpose of this study was to provide recommendations to the leadership team at Hampton High School with possible solutions to the problem of students' low test scores on the Ohio Educational Assessment (OEA) for Science. This introduction provides information regarding the organizational profile, an introduction to the problem and its significance, along with the purpose of the study. The central research question is presented, and this section of the report closes with a list of key terms with definitions.

Writing an Overview Section

The first piece of information required for the Overview is a brief restatement of the purpose of the research. The second piece of information required for the Overview is an introduction to the contents of the information that will be presented in this section of the report. For example, in the Introduction section, the Overview will introduce the reader to the organizational profile, an introduction to the problem, the significance of the problem, the purpose statement, the central research question and the definitions. An Overview will be written for each section of the educational report. Please refer to the requirements given in the checklist that follows and apply these requirements to each of the Overview sections of the educational report.

Checklist for an Overview

☐ Does the Overview include the purpose of the research?
☐ Does the Overview introduce the major headings of the section?

Organizational Profile

The **Organizational Profile** provides the reader with context for the problem. This portion of the educational report includes the nature and history of the organization.

See Organizational Profile example below:

Organizational Profile

The educational site for this study was a suburban public high school in southeastern Ohio. The mission of Hampton High School is to "provide learning opportunities in a safe environment and to help students acquire skills and knowledge necessary to become life-long learners." Hampton High School serves four townships and 859 students. The school is predominantly Caucasian with 7% minority enrollment. Thirty-two percent of the student body is considered economically disadvantaged. A total of 63 teachers serve the school, resulting in a 14:1 student-to-teacher ratio. School administrators include a principal and two assistant principals and a Director of Student Services. For this study, the school's science department was the focus. The science department comprises nine teachers and offers a total of 17 courses. Within the department, leadership is shared among four science teachers who, when responsibilities are combined, function as a department chair. Instructional decisions, including which science courses are taught and the standards associated within these courses, are generally determined among the four science teachers within the department with oversight by an assistant principal.

Writing an Organizational Profile Section

The Organizational Profile should include the educational site in which the problem will be addressed and information pertaining to that site. In this section, the site of the project should be described in detail (e.g., geographic location, demographic information, school system, mission statement [objectives], faculty and/or staff, programs, services, public or private, etc.). For example, you may say, "Washington Middle School is located at 000 Main Street, Springfield, Virginia. The school serves 000 students … and is …" When writing this section, it is important to give a detailed description of the school or educational setting. If relevant, consider weaving in the history of the organization.

Checklist for the Organizational Profile

- ☐ Does the Organizational Profile include the educational site?
- ☐ Does the Organizational Profile include whether the organization is public or private?
- ☐ Does the Organizational Profile include the geographic location?
- ☐ Does the Organizational Profile include the mission statement?
- ☐ Does the Organizational Profile include demographic information?
- ☐ Does the Organizational Profile include a description of the faculty and/or staff?
- ☐ Does the Organizational Profile include a description of programs and services, if applicable?
- ☐ The Organizational Profile is written in paragraph format.
- ☐ The Organizational Profile is written in past tense.

Introduction to the Problem

In this section of the educational report, you will introduce the reader to the problem of practice. A **problem of practice** is any identified educational area that focuses on processes or practices that are observable and measurable and that may be improved upon or solved. Most educators are familiar with several issues that are problematic and would like to see improved. As the researcher, you will need to work closely with the site's leadership to discuss any problems that need a solution or practices that need to be improved. This may require several meetings before you can define the problem. During this process, you need to narrow the discussion to a specific problem. Keep in mind that you cannot solve all the known problems through the research process. The scope of your research needs to be reasonable. For instance, if the problem of practice that you want to solve is drug abuse among students at a school, it may be best to focus on a particular type of drug abuse, such as underage drinking, rather than drug abuse in general. Furthermore, using the example of drug abuse, applied research is site-specific and is not intended to solve drug abuse for all high school students in the United States, as the scope of that population is simply too large. However, if a high school in your locality has a problem with underage drinking, this may be a logical research topic since this may be a problem of practice that could be solved or improved for that specific school. Educational research can be an effective way to help make improvements in practice based on data collected and analyzed, and recommend relevant solutions, as long as the problem in practice is logical for the specific site chosen.

See Introduction to the Problem example below:

Introduction to the Problem

The problem is that approximately half of the students at Hampton High School have failed to meet the state's level of satisfactory performance on the Ohio Educational Assessment (OEA) for Science (ODOE, 2020a). Over the last three academic years, approximately 50% of students failed to meet the ODOE's expectations (ODOE, 2020b). Specifically, low expectations are defined as students' performance that "demonstrates an incomplete understanding of essential concepts in science and inconsistent connections among central ideas" (ODOE, 2018b, p. 14). Students scoring below 50% on the test are considered to have failed the science assessment (ODOE, 2018b). Low scores on the assessment have had a detrimental effect on Hampton High School and have reflected poorly on students, parents, teachers, staff, and administrators, as well as the school board, town governments, and businesses and companies within the region. In the past, the school has tried to solve this problem by requiring teachers to spend more time teaching concepts covered on the test. Most recently, the school has offered free after-school tutoring for students. Both historically and presently, these efforts have not proven effective, as approximately half of the students who take the assessment fail.

Writing an Introduction to the Problem Section

The Introduction should begin with a clear statement of the problem. For example, "The problem is that approximately half of the students at Hampton High School have failed to meet the state's level of satisfactory performance on the Ohio Educational Assessment for Science" (ODOE, n.d.). Once you have the introductory sentence, support the statement by citing facts and statistics. Lay out a convincing case using solid evidence that the problem does, in fact, exist. For example, you could write, "Over the last three academic years, approximately 50% of students failed to meet the ODOE's expectations (ODOE, n.d.). Then include what has been done in the past and what is currently being done to solve the problem.

A word of caution for every educator who desires to conduct research: It is easy to be disgruntled with a problem that exists in your school, district, or locality. An educational research study is not a platform to use to justify or vocalize dissatisfaction with current practice. The information you collect during your research should lend to solving the problem, furthering understanding, or reporting evidence, and not justifying perceived poor practice. As the researcher, you need to be a part of the solution and not a part of the problem. Below are several examples of problems of practice that may potentially lend to an appropriate applied research study in an educational setting.

- Low science scores on standardized assessments
- Lack of parental involvement in after-school activities
- Teacher absenteeism
- High incidence of student behavior referrals dealing with disrespect
- Limited professional development opportunities in gifted education
- Poorly implemented remedial math instruction
- Third grade reading comprehension

There are a multitude of problems and practices in education that can be solved or improved. The key to defining a problem is using evidence to reveal the problem and to determine an appropriate and practical scope of the problem.

Checklist for Introduction to the Problem

- ☐ Does the Introduction to the Problem begin with the problem statement?
- ☐ Does the Introduction to the Problem include supporting evidence (statistics, facts)?
- ☐ Does the Introduction to the Problem include what was done in the past to solve the problem?
- ☐ Does the Introduction to the Problem include what is currently being done to solve the problem?
- ☐ The Introduction is written in paragraph format.
- ☐ The Introduction to the Problem is written in past tense.

Significance of the Problem

The **Significance of the Problem** is defined as the practical contributions that the research makes to the organization or stakeholders. It is important to specify why the research is necessary and how the research may improve the educational experience. This section will state how the research is significant and who it is significant to. Consider the following questions:

- Who will benefit from this information?
- What difference will this research make?
- Is this a timely study or one that has been over-researched?
- Why will you conduct this research?
- Where will you be allowed to conduct the research?
- How will your study contribute to solving a problem?

These are all important questions to consider when determining the significance of your study and narrowing down the topic for your research. Let's look at each of these questions in a little more detail.

Who will benefit from this information?

The benefactors could be administrators, teachers, counselors, students, parents, district-level leaders, heads of state, military families, students with special needs, gifted students, rural districts, or almost any other stakeholders in a problem. For the purpose of applied research, you will need to clearly define, as much as is possible, the stakeholders who *may* benefit from your study. Notice that the word "may" is used. This is intentional, as you do not know, and you cannot predict, who "will" benefit from the research, but you can state who *may* benefit.

What difference will this research make?

Clearly articulate this difference in order to truly present the fact that your study could solve a problem and possibly make a difference for the stakeholders of the study. The intent of applied research is to offer a *possible* solution to a real-world problem. Again, you are not offering THE solution to the problem in practice; rather, you are suggesting a POSSIBLE solution. You want your research to make a difference, but you cannot guarantee that it will make a difference.

Is this a timely study or one that has been over-researched?

Timeliness is important as educational practices are constantly changing. When the idea of teaching students by using computers was first introduced, it became a highly researched topic. Today, research is not necessary to determine whether or not teaching students with computers is effective, but the multitude of programs and methods used to teach students with computers is still a relevant and timely topic, as this is an ever-changing and a rapidly-growing area of education.

Where will you be allowed to conduct research?

In order to conduct applied research, you must have approval from the gatekeepers at the location where you intend to conduct your study. Will you have access to the participants that you will need for your study? It is not enough to know of a problem in practice at a particular school (or other location); you also need permission to conduct the research at that particular school/location from the person (or persons) who has the authority to make the decision about whether you will be allowed to conduct your research there.

Why will you conduct this research?

What is your motivation for conducting your study? Examine your motives to make sure they are ethical and that they will lend themselves to making improvements in practice.

How will your study contribute to solving a problem?

Solving a problem in practice is the intended outcome of applied research. Is your problem in practice worthy of research? Your topic needs to be relevant and specific in order to solve a meaningful problem in practice.

See Significance of the Problem example below:

Significance of the Problem

The benefits of improving students' performance on the Ohio Educational Assessment (OEA) for Science include extrinsic aspects, such as scholarship and college placement opportunities for students (Ellis, 2018), as well as more intrinsic benefits, including an increased sense of pride and ability. For stakeholders, including teachers and administrators, increased scores on the OEA for Science may lead to increased teacher efficacy, which studies have shown lead to even greater instructional practices (Ware, 2002). An increase in test scores may be seen as a positive indicator on teacher evaluations. Administrators benefit from increased test scores by allowing them to shift their focus on other initiatives within the school, which may lead to increased funding and community support. When students' achievement is high, the school is likely to boast a higher rating among other schools. This can translate to a more desirable community in which to live, increasing property values, attracting businesses and companies, increasing local revenue, employment opportunities, and making the community an ideal location for graduates to live (Lynch, 2015).

Writing the Significance of the Problem Section

The significance of the problem begins with a description of the practical contributions that the project makes to the organization or stakeholders. It addresses questions such as: Why does the problem need to be solved? Why it is important to the location, organization, population, and/or stakeholders? How might solving the problem improve the conditions, lives, work environment, etc.? Identify the specific stakeholders who may find the project beneficial. References based on the literature are very important here; they are vital to support the need for the study. All assertions in this subsection must be supported by the literature and citations must be used.

Checklist for Significance of the Problem

☐ Does the Significance of the Problem include a description of the practical contributions the project makes to the stakeholders and organization?

☐ Does the Significance of the Problem include how the research could improve educational conditions for the community at large?

☐ Does the Significance of the Problem include citations to support assertions?

☐ The Significance of the Problem is written in paragraph format.

☐ The Significance of the Problem is written in past tense.

Purpose Statement

The **purpose statement** introduces the reader to the specific purpose of the study. The purpose of the research should be to solve a problem or improve a practice. This information should be communicated in a concisely written problem statement.

See Purpose Statement example below:

Purpose Statement

The purpose of this study is to provide recommendations to the leadership team at Hampton High School with possible solutions to the problem of students' low test scores on the Ohio Educational Assessment (OEA) for Science. This applied research study used both qualitative and quantitative data collection approaches. The first approach used structured interviews with a total of five participants from Hampton High science teachers and one administrator. Each of these participants is familiar with the OEA for Science and students' historical performance on the assessment. The second approach employed a survey of teachers in the science department, two special education collaborative teachers for the science department, the school's testing coordinator and counselor, a retired department chair with 30 years of experience at the school, and four administrators at Hampton High School. This survey was administered using Google Forms, a web-based platform hosted by Google. The third approach utilized a review of documents from the ODOE focusing on Hampton High School students' performance over the last three years on the OEA.

Writing the Purpose Statement Section

Begin this section by stating the specific purpose of the study. There is no need to change this format since it is specific and to the point. The purpose is either to solve a problem or to improve a practice or issue. You will notice after reading the next section that each purpose statement below is directly related to the central research question associated with the study. Discussion of the central research question follows this section; thus, the purpose statement methodically leads directly into the central research question. The purpose of the study and the central research question must be written using the exact same verbiage throughout the paper since the purpose and central research question do not change.

Central Research Question

- How can the problem of (<u>identify the problem</u>) be solved?

Purpose Statement

- The purpose of this study is to provide recommendations to solve the problem of _____.

OR

Central Research Question

- How can (<u>practice or issue</u>) be improved?

Purpose Statement

- The purpose of this study is to improve _____.

Checklist for Purpose Statement

☐ Does the Purpose Statement section follow the template for the purpose statement?

☐ Does the Purpose Statement section include the data collection approaches?

☐ Does the Purpose Statement section include details related to each approach (participants, documents, artifacts, etc.)?

☐ The Purpose Statement is written in paragraph format.

☐ The Purpose Statement is written in past tense.

Central Research Question

The research question is one of the most important elements of a research study; it will guide your study and help to keep the research focused. The **central research question** is the research question that you seek to answer through the data collection and data analysis processes.

See Central Research Question example below:

Central Research Question

How can the problem of students' low test scores on the Ohio Educational

Assessment for Science be solved at Hampton High School?

Writing the Central Research Question

The central research question for your study should be derived from the problem and purpose statements. A well-written central question is practical, clear, significant, and ethical. The central research question gives guidance and parameters for your research. Choose one of the following two formats.

Central Research Question

■ How can the problem of <u>(identify the problem)</u> be solved?

OR

Central Research Question

■ How can <u>(practice or issue)</u> be improved?

The central research question is meant to be a short question that should be addressed by the research. The central research question gives guidance and parameters to the research. For example, if your central research question is "How can the problem of bullying be solved?", your research would not include topics outside of the realm of bullying, such as teacher attendance, unless documented bullying incidences increased when a classroom teacher was absent. This central research question should guide you to adhering to the specific topic of bullying while considering the following questions:

■ What is the cause of the problem?

■ What are the prior solutions to the problem?

■ What is currently being done to solve the problem?

■ How would the researcher solve the problem based on the literature review and data collection and analysis?

You will use the information you gathered when answering the central research question to determine and address the recommendations later in the educational report.

Checklist for the Central Research Question

☐ Is the Central Research Question derived from the problem and purpose statements?

☐ Does the Central Research Question follow one of the two formats provided in the Central Research Question section of this textbook?

Definitions

For an applied research study in education, the **definitions** are terms that are relevant to the study and that are designated in the educational report. These terms are defined using the scholarly literature.
See Definitions example below:

Definitions

1. *Accountability* – "the process of evaluating school performance on the basis of student performance measures" (Loeb & Figlio, 2011, para. 1).

2. *Accreditation* – "a process by which recognized authorities validate that an institution meets minimal professional standards and accountability based on its mission" (Greenberg, 2014, p. 2).

Writing the Definitions

Writing the definitions for an educational report is meant to be straightforward and scholarly. Terms that are relevant to the study should be included. It is important to also include terms that use abbreviations and include those abbreviations. Dictionary definitions are not acceptable. For example, a definition using the literature could look like one of the following:

Attitude—Attitude is a psychological tendency that involves evaluating a particular object with some degree of favor or disfavor (Eagly & Chaiken, 2007).

Interest—The combination of emotion and personal valuation of a task resulting in a desire for various levels of enjoyment (Ainley & Ainley, 2011).

There is not a set number of terms that you should include in your educational report, but as a general rule, words that are used in the study, but are not commonly known, should be defined. Also, words that are used frequently in the report, but may have multiple known definitions should be defined. For example, if you state that students at Hampton High School have been bullied, the term bullied, as used in your study, should be clearly defined. Otherwise, the term may be misinterpreted by the reader based on his or her own general knowledge of bullying.

Checklist for the Definitions

☐ Do the Definitions include all terms relevant to the study?

☐ Are the Definitions defined using the literature and not a dictionary?

☐ Are the Definitions cited?

☐ Are Definitions presented in list format?

Conclusion

A well-written Introduction to the study introduces the reader to the topic of the research and the problem to be solved; it includes enough detail so that the reader has a thorough idea of what the study is about as well as who stands to benefit from the research. The Introduction includes the organizational profile, which details the site where the research will be conducted with demographic and other information. An introduction to the problem and the significance of the problem are written in detail, as well as the purpose statement, the central research question, and the definitions related to the research. This section of the educational report is essential for communicating more detail about the research than is disclosed in the front matter.

Chapter Highlights

The Introduction to the study is the section that introduces the reader to the topic of the research and the problem to be solved.

The Introduction includes the Organizational Profile, an Introduction to the Problem, the Significance of the Problem, the Purpose Statement, the Central Research Question, and Definitions related to the research.

The Organizational Profile provides the reader with context for the problem. This section includes the educational setting, the nature, and history of the organization used in the study.

The problem of practice is introduced and explained in the Introduction to the Problem section.

The problem of practice needs to be reasonable, well-defined, and have a possible solution.

The problem of practice is often determined and defined in a coordinated effort between the researcher and leadership and/or stakeholders.

The problem is introduced in a clear statement of the problem. The problem needs to be supported by facts and statistics that demonstrate it is a problem.

The Significance of the Problem section specifies why research related to the stated problem is necessary and how the research may improve the educational experience. This section will also state how the research is significant and to whom the research is significant. This section begins with a description of practical contributions that are based on cited literature.

The purpose statement introduces the reader to the specific purpose of the study. The purpose of the research should be to solve a problem or improve a practice.

The central research question is one of the most important elements of a research study in that it guides the study.

A well-written central question is practical, clear, significant, and ethical.

Terms relevant to the study and their definitions are included.

The definitions are not dictionary definitions; the definitions are written based on how the terms are defined in scholarly literature.

The definitions need to be clear, straightforward, and scholarly. Abbreviations are also included and defined in this section.

CHAPTER 4

Writing a Literature Review for an Educational Report

Chapter Outline

Introduction
The Overview
Narrative Review
A Strategic Approach to Writing a Literature Review
A Strategic Approach to Analyzing and Synthesizing Scholarly Works
A Strategic Approach to Writing a Literature Review
Conclusion

Objectives

By the end of this chapter, the reader will be able to:

- Describe the peer review process
- List the sections in the literature review of an educational report
- Explain purposes of a literature review
- Differentiate between primary and secondary sources
- List aspects of writing that are important to consider when writing a literature review
- Demonstrate procedures for locating scholarly sources
- Identify scholarly sources
- Develop a system for organizing information for a literature review
- Explain the difference between a summary of published literature and a synthesis of published literature
- Develop a basic outline for a literature review

Key Terms

- Peer-review process
- The Overview
- Primary source
- Secondary source
- Author's voice
- Topic sentence

Introduction

A formal literature review should be approached strategically to ensure a high-quality review of the current literature that includes an analysis and synthesis of known research, knowledge, and thinking that precedes the proposed research. The purpose of a formal literature review is to advance the author's knowledge about a problem of practice or specific topic and to present the formal literature review as a justification, or argument, for conducting research and to provide the researcher with enough information to make an informed decision regarding the recommendations to improve educational practices. The formal literature review provides the context for research and demonstrates the importance of the research based on the current literature. To compose a quality literature review, hundreds, or even thousands, of peer-reviewed scholarly journal articles may need to be read and analyzed. According to the American Psychological Association (APA, 2020), the **peer-review process** is the process when a potential journal article manuscript is reviewed and evaluated by the authors' peers in the scientific community based on the quality and potential contribution of each article. Peer-reviewed articles in the literature review should represent the latest findings about a proposed problem of practice or research topic.

The review of literature is often the longest portion of the educational report, and it usually ranges from 15 to 30 pages, but it may be longer. This review of the literature is not simply a study-by-study summary, but it is a selection of relevant literature that covers a specific topic and related research studies. As you read the literature, the information relevant to your project will need to be categorized into major themes that will be presented using headings arranged in a logical order. The literature review communicates what has been examined on the topic, what empirical studies have been conducted, and what solutions have been implemented to address the problem. As you write the literature review, you may weave a theoretical component into the paper, including the theorist(s), if you discover a dominant theory while reviewing the literature. The theoretical component will not be a separate section, but, if included, it will be used to explain your proposed research topic. Examples of theoretical components include Maslow's (1943) hierarchy of needs, Bandura's (1997) self-efficacy theory, etc. You must explain the relationship between the theory and your proposed study. This chapter offers a step-by-step process for writing a review of the current scholarly literature for an applied research project and includes the Overview, Narrative Review, and Summary.

 Go to *www.khlearn.com* to watch a video about getting started on a literature review.

The Overview

Begin the literature review with the Overview section. The **Overview** includes the first paragraph(s) of the literature review and it introduces the reader to the broad topics addressed in the review of the literature. This section should be somewhat brief and should mention the problem and purpose of the study and then introduce the main headings (the main topics) of the literature review.

See Overview example below:

Overview

The purpose of this study was to provide recommendations to the leadership team at Hampton High School with possible solutions to the problem of students' low test scores on the Ohio Educational Assessment (OEA) for Science. This portion of the report examines literature related to the research problem. The historical significance of standardized testing is discussed, along with its evolution into modern educational practices. Additionally, the OEA for Science is discussed in detail, particularly with regard to how this test was designed and developed, as well as its manner of fulfilling federal accountability requirements. Finally, factors that are associated with students' performance on standardized tests are discussed.

Narrative Review

The purpose of the literature review is to justify the rationale for the problem and position the study within the existing knowledge base on the topic (Creswell & Poth, 2018). The literature review should present the justification or argument for your proposed problem of practice or research topic and should help you determine possible solutions or recommendations for the problem you are researching. The literature review is not merely a collection of citations from multiple journal articles; it is a synthesis of the information that has been previously published. The impetus for your research must be well-established, and the rationale for the research must be thoroughly grounded in the literature. The presentation of the content of the literature review is critical to support the justification for the research. Research studies and other scholarly information presented in the literature review must be analyzed and synthesized with other relevant studies, and the literature review must demonstrate a clear connection between prior research and your proposed research.

Writing a literature review will require a lot of time; this is not a paper that will (or should) be written quickly. Gall et al. (1996) estimated that the completion of an acceptable literature review will take between 3 and 6 months of time and effort; some may take longer. When a literature review is complete, you should know how the topic of research began, how it evolved over time, what research studies further informed the topic, how thought patterns have changed about the topic based on current research, and the criticisms and debates associated with the topic. In essence, you, the author of the literature review, should become a scholar or expert on the research topic. A thorough review of the literature, coupled with data collection and analysis from the proposed research, should enable you to make logical recommendations to help improve an educational practice.

Purposes of a Literature Review include:

- To disclose historical aspects of the problem of practice or topic
- To demonstrate the factors that may impact the problem of practice or topic
- To convey an argument for the proposed research
- To present a critical synthesis and analysis of the existing literature
- To establish the state of previous research to disclose how the new research may advance the previous research
- To demonstrate the researcher's critical analysis and knowledge about the problem of practice or topic

Questions that are specifically answered through the literature:

- What does the literature say about the problem?
- What is the cause of the problem of practice?

- What are the prior solutions to the problem?
- How does the literature solve the problem?
- How would you, as the researcher, solve the problem?

All of the above questions should be addressed in the literature review using peer-reviewed journal articles and other scholarly sources. These questions will not be answered as given, per say, but each question will be addressed as you develop the major headings, or topics, of your literature review.

Primary and secondary sources should be used for writing the literature review. **Primary sources** are publications written by an individual or individuals who actually conducted the research or work that is published. An example of a primary source is a journal article that presents results of research an author or authors conducted. If the article in the journal was presented as an opinion or evaluation of research conducted by others, it would be considered a secondary source. **Secondary sources** are works or publications in which the author or authors review educational practices and programs or research studies conducted by others about a problem of practice or research topic.

Primary sources should make up the majority of your cited work, though some secondary sources are appropriate. Remember that primary sources are written by the author(s) of the actual research; those authors have first-hand knowledge about the research because they conducted it and are able to provide more detailed information than a secondary author or source could write about that same research. Again, scholarly peer-reviewed works should be included in a literature review.

Gall et al. (1996) stated that another reason for conducting a formal literature review is to "initiate planning for your own research" (p. 51). This is precisely what you will do. Though there are multiple other logical reasons for conducting a literature review, the applied research literature review will focus on the above reasons. When writing the literature review outline, these guiding purposes will decrease the chances that the literature review will appear convoluted and disjointed. Rudestam and Newtons (2007) noted several important aspects of writing that are important to remember to compose a quality literature review.

Be a Convincing Writer: Remember that the literature review provides the context for the proposed research and demonstrates why the topic requires additional research. The literature review must demonstrate the relationship between previous research and the proposed study. It must also communicate how the research is different from existing research.

Be a Critic Not a Reporter: Present a critical analysis of the relationships among research articles. The literature review should **not** be a collection of facts; rather, it should present a coherent argument that leads to the problem statement or topic of the study. The literature review should begin with a clear statement of the research goal and should be followed by a structured argument for the research. Direct quotations should rarely be used in a literature review.

Be a Selective Writer: Be selective about the articles chosen to include in the literature review; discuss only the most relevant articles. More than 2,000 journal articles may be reviewed for a literature review, but only a fraction of those will be included in the actual literature review. Choose only the best articles that are relevant to your proposed study. This means that you must be intentional about which articles to include and exclude from the literature review.

Be a Skillful Researcher: In your literature review, use primarily seminal articles and articles that were recently published in the literature review. Always strive to cite scholarly, primary sources that are reputable. Approximately 85% to 90% of the scholarly articles included in the literature review should have been published within the last five years; otherwise, the research may be considered outdated.

Be a Reasonable Problem Solver: At the conclusion of the literature review, write a paragraph or section that highlights the most relevant literature and the conclusions that led to the proposed study.

A well-written literature review reflects data collection, analysis, interpretation, and conclusions that are beneficial beyond the current study. The quality of the literature review establishes your credibility as a researcher and author; thus, the presentation, organization, and inclusion and exclusion of information must be intentional and must be scholarly.

 Go to *www.khlearn.com* to watch a video about composing a literature review.

A Strategic Approach to Writing a Literature Review

Begin your literature review by locating, reading, and analyzing scholarly journal articles and books. In order to begin this process, you must be able to distinguish scholarly works from other types of information.

How to Locate Scholarly Sources

Reviewing literature involves searching, browsing, skimming, reading, saving, and organizing scholarly works that are relevant to your proposed problem of practice or topic. The Internet is the fastest and most effective way to locate scholarly sources. If you are enrolled as a student or work for a college or university, it is likely that you have free access to excellent sources of scholarly works through services such as Ebsco Host and ProQuest. Many colleges and universities have subscriptions to these services that offer several options for searching for scholarly sources. Other ways of searching for scholarly sources include Google Scholar, ERIC, Oxford Reference Online, and Britannica Online. Many library databases offer the option to limit search results to include only peer-reviewed articles, which is a very helpful tool for locating scholarly, peer-reviewed journal articles. Always use that option when it is available. When searching using Google Scholar or similar sources, payment might be expected for access to the articles. If that happens, one option is to enter the title, author, DOI, or other information about the article into the search engine for the library at your institution. If the article is available at your institution's library, you will not have to PAY to access the entire article. Some colleges and universities will also obtain a copy of the article for you if they do not have it in their database. Many other articles are available and may be located with a simple Google search, though many of the results will require payment for access to the full article. Note that Wikipedia is not considered a scholarly source, in most cases, and it should not be cited in academic work such as a capstone project, thesis, or dissertation. Wikipedia is a good source for learning a quick tidbit of information, but for the purposes of scholarly writing, Wikipedia information should be verified by a scholarly source. When searching for scholarly sources, look for the following items:

Author or authors are identified

Publisher is identified

Citations within the text

References follow the text

Though this is not a fool-proof means of identifying scholarly works, it may help eliminate many non-scholarly works. Remember that not everything posted on the internet is accurate or scholarly, thus discernment must play a role in locating scholarly sources.

Searching for Peer-Reviewed Journal Articles

To help begin the search for peer-reviewed articles, consider this example using the stated central research question for applied research.

Central Question: How can the problem of low test scores on the Ohio Educational Assessment for Science be solved at Hampton High School?

In a search engine, such as Google Scholar, you could use any of the following words and phrases to begin your search since these are the main topics in the central research question:

- Low-test scores
- Ohio Educational Assessment
- Science assessment

A search including the three aforementioned topics will yield a lot of information; this information alone may be overwhelming. Let's look again at the three main ideas from the central research question and add limitations to the search so as to yield more specific scholarly publications. Note that each of the main ideas may have multiple limiting identifiers.

Low-test scores
  Low assessment scores
  Failing test scores
  Assessment failure
  Failing student test scores

Ohio Educational Assessment
  OEA
  Standardized tests
  Standardized assessments
  Failing standardized tests
  Poor student performance on standardized tests
  Poor student performance on assessments

Science Assessment
  Evidence-based science strategies
  Evidence-based teaching strategies
  Science strategies
  Science assessments

The list for limiting the search on the topic of low test scores on the Ohio Educational Assessment for Science could continue, as there are a multitude of ways that these terms can be searched. These may also be further limited by date, such as articles published within the past five years or by author if a specific author is preferred. This list of specific parameters provides an effective start to the search for scholarly publications regarding the central research question, which was, "How can the problem of low test scores on the Ohio Educational Assessment for Science be solved at Hampton High School?"

 Go to *www.khlearn.com* to watch a video about organizing information.

Organizing Information

Organizing information is a critical component of writing an effective literature review. From the very beginning of your search for scholarly sources, you should establish a system to organize the scholarly articles that you review. One recommendation is to create files on your desktop. The files could include a variety of headings and could be organized by topic, author, date, or other options. The folders on your desktop for the topic of low OEA scores could look like this:

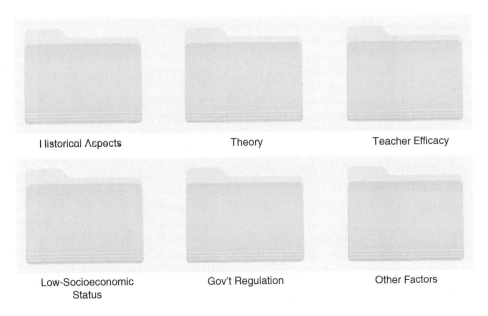

| Historical Aspects | Theory | Teacher Efficacy |
| Low-Socioeconomic Status | Gov't Regulation | Other Factors |

Folders © Mastak A/Shutterstock.com

This is only one way to organize journal articles. Some researchers have a combination of paper and digital copies. Determine an effective way to organize the information you gather so that you can easily retrieve the information when needed. The most effective way to do this is to set up a system of organization at the onset of your research. It is easy to lose information or forget where you saved or filed the information unless you establish and implement an organized method for storage and retrieval.

Another recommended tool is to make one long, comprehensive list of references starting at the very beginning of the searching process. If your institution requires a specific format (such as APA, MLA, Turabian, etc.), create the list of references in that particular format from the beginning. Making a list of all references that you have read will help in several ways, including the following:

1. If you create a list of articles that you have read, you will not accidentally read an article twice without remembrance. This will save you time.

2. If you have a list of references, you can make a quick note or label beside each reference. These labels could include short terms of reference such as: Theory, Teacher Efficacy, Include quote, Do not use, Excellent, SES, Govt., etc. These labels can then be used to help you quickly identify and retrieve articles that pertain to your outline headings. Creating a reference list with labels makes for a quick storage and retrieval process.

3. When you create a reference list at the beginning of your search, the list will indicate how many articles you have read or accessed. Though the quantity of journal articles read does not determine the quality of the work, it will give you an idea of how many articles you have read on the topic.

4. When a reference list is created from the beginning of the search, it is easier to compile a reference list as you read each article than it is to try to go back and find an article. When possible, include an active hyperlink to each article. Including an active hyperlink to the article makes it extremely easy to find and retrieve the article when needed.

Another recommendation for organizing information for a literature review is to write an annotated bibliography. To write an annotated bibliography, select the highlights of each article (or other source) and write an appraisal of each source. Start with the citation you will use in the reference list and write down key ideas the author(s) presented and other important information in the article.

As you read and organize scholarly works, consider the information presented and determine how you will present this collection of information. Having a plan in place for organizing and retrieving the information is important when you are dealing with this large quantity of information.

Assembling the Information

Composing a literature review begins with a system or a plan for incorporating the vast amount of information that you have read and organized. Formulating and writing an outline is an effective way to approach the literature review to ensure that your literature review is well-organized and that your thoughts flow smoothly. This outline will obviously need to be revised throughout the writing process as you collect new information, but this is how an effective literature review will develop from the massive amount of information read, collected, and organized. As you insert information into the outline, you will begin to see the literature review develop. As you assemble the information into an outline, revisit the purposes for writing a literature review as noted below.

- To disclose historical aspects of the problem of practice or topic
- To demonstrate the factors that may impact the problem of practice or topic
- To convey an argument for the proposed research
- To present a critical synthesis and analysis of the existing literature
- To establish the state of previous research to disclose how the new research may advance the previous research
- To demonstrate the researcher's critical analysis and knowledge about the problem of practice or topic

All the concepts regarding the purposes of the literature review need to be incorporated within, or woven into, the fabric of your literature review. Below is an example of a very small section of a literature review. Read the example below and decide if it seems like an acceptable section based on the information presented thus far in this chapter.

Key Factors for Success of Students with ASD in Higher Education

Peña and Kocur (2013) affirmed that college is not only an attainable goal for students with autism spectrum disorder (ASD), but it may also be important to their growth in other ways. Gobbo and Shmulsky (2014) stated that "attaining a college degree is a formidable challenge for many individuals with disabilities who enroll in postsecondary institutions at a rate close to that of the general population but earn fewer credits and degrees" (p. 13). The literature revealed that students with ASD struggle to make the transition from high school to the university setting and face both academic and non-academic challenges (Wehman et al., 2014; Wei et al., 2015). Oftentimes the support services in higher education are insufficient and uncoordinated (White et al., 2011) or are not specific to students with ASD (Mitchell & Beresford, 2014).

Adapted from Claxton, B. L. (2016). A case study of an office of disability support services in higher education for students with autism spectrum disorder (Publication No. 10170156) (Doctoral dissertation). ProQuest Dissertations & Theses Global, Liberty University, Lynchburg, VA.

Based on the purposes of the literature and the guidelines given thus far in this chapter, the above section is not an acceptable paragraph for a formal literature review. This paragraph is merely a collection of citations from a review of the literature, and it is not a critical analysis of the literature. Another reason that this paragraph is not acceptable is that the researcher neglected to insert his or her voice in the paragraph. This paragraph does not establish the author as being part of the literature review, and it certainly does not present the author as a scholar on the topic of key factors for students with ASD in higher education.

Let's look at an improved and acceptable version of the paragraph. Again, note that this is just a small example to help you understand and establish the difference in an effective and ineffective literature review.

Key Factors for Success of Students with ASD in Higher Education

Though some believe that college is an unattainable goal for students with special needs, Peña and Kocur (2013) affirmed that college is not only an attainable goal for students with ASD, but it may also be important for their growth in other ways such as real-world experiences and social and emotional understandings. Many students with ASD aspire to earn a college degree; however, Gobbo and Shmulsky (2014) stated that "attaining a college degree is a formidable challenge for many individuals with disabilities, who enroll in postsecondary institutions at a rate close to that of the general population but earn fewer credits and degrees" (p. 13). It is this challenge that needs to be further researched, as many students with ASD desire a college degree but are unsure of how to meet the challenges associated with this achievement. Transitioning from a supportive high school environment to the unknown in a university setting presents challenges for all students, but it is especially challenging for those with ASD who are accustomed to the supports offered through their IEPs in the high school setting. The literature reveals that students with ASD struggle to make the transition from high school to the university setting and face both academic and non-academic challenges (Wehman, 2014; Wei et al., 2015). Though some universities offer support services to assist students with disabilities, oftentimes the support services are insufficient and uncoordinated (White et al., 2011) or are not specific to students with ASD (Mitchell & Beresford, 2014). These limiting factors for students with ASD need to be explored further to determine a solution to the problem of factors that hinder students with ASD from being successful in a post-secondary setting.

Adapted from Claxton, B. L. (2016). A case study of an office of disability support services in higher education for students with autism spectrum disorder (Publication No. 10170156) (Doctoral dissertation). ProQuest Dissertations & Theses Global, Liberty University, Lynchburg, VA.

Note that the writer's voice may be heard in sentences such as:

- Some believe that college is an unattainable goal for students with special needs.
- Many students with ASD aspire to earn a college degree.
- It is this challenge that needs to be addressed, as many students with ASD desire a college degree, but are unsure of how to meet the challenges associated with this achievement. Transitioning from a supportive high school environment to the unknown in a university setting presents challenges for all students, but especially for those with ASD who are accustomed to the supports offered through their IEP in the high school setting.
- Some universities offer support services to assist students with disabilities.
- These limiting factors for students with ASD need to be explored further to determine a solution to the problem of factors that hinder students with ASD from being successful in a post-secondary setting.

Though this is a *very* brief example, it serves the purpose of distinguishing between a collection of citations and a critical analysis and synthesis of the literature. This is oftentimes referred to as hearing the **author's voice**. Writing an effective literature review and establishing oneself as a scholar on a specific problem of practice or topic requires that the author's voice be heard throughout the literature review since this serves as the justification for the author's proposed research. In order to interject "voice" into the literature review, you must learn how to evaluate, analyze, and synthesize scholarly works, and write that information in your review of the literature.

Go to *www.khlearn.com* to watch a video about assembling information.

A Strategic Approach to Analyzing and Synthesizing Scholarly Works

Before a research study can begin, researchers need a complete, clear, and comprehensive understanding of the problem being addressed to include the characteristics of the topic, the impetus of the study, and the information being desired (Bickman & Rog, 2009). The literature review is a process where you synthesize current research and scholarly literature to identify historical aspects of the topic, common trends, and current implications of the proposed research. The literature review should address the cause or causes of the problem or topic, elaborate on the current state of the literature regarding the problem or topic, and present prior solutions to the problem or research questions. A well-written literature review will thoroughly address all three of these areas by analyzing and synthesizing the current state of the literature.

A poorly written literature review will present a collection of information from the abstracts of articles and/or the results sections of the articles. Information presented from only the abstract and results sections of journal articles does not present a valid justification for a research study; it merely states the results of what other researchers have accomplished. A solid literature review will note specific details of scholarly journal articles, such as data collection procedures, sample size, data analysis procedures, the participants, the context in which the information was presented, and conclusions drawn. Additionally, to write a thorough literature review, you will need to consider the trustworthiness, dependability, validity, and objectivity of each article and explain such considerations within the literature review as being noteworthy. You may also present the strengths and limitations of the study in relation to your proposed problem or topic.

As the researcher, it is your moral obligation to critically read and evaluate each source. A strategic method to accomplish this is to complete the template below (or similar one) for every scholarly source you consider for the literature review. The key to effectively accomplishing this is to determine the valid and relevant information in each article. Below, you will find a strategic approach to analyzing and synthesizing scholarly publications.

Journal articles must be analyzed individually, and they must be analyzed and synthesized collectively. This means that, for each peer-reviewed journal article, the following two steps should be completed:

First: Complete the **Individual Scholarly Works Review** template.

Second: Complete the **Comparative Scholarly Works Review** template

The comparison of scholarly works presents your voice, your argument, and your justification for the research. Doing this comparison is the key to writing an effective literature review. As you complete the template for this step of the literature review process, note that it is important to report the data as found, and this includes sources that offer a divergent perspective, if one is found in a review of the current literature, otherwise, your review of the literature will be incomplete. Without this comparative analysis and synthesis, your literature review will result in a simple collection of ideas without an effective argument and justification for the research.

Individual Scholarly Works Template

Title of the scholarly work:
Is this a journal article, book, or other?
Is it peer-reviewed?
What is(are) the major topic(s) presented?
Which words are repeated often?
How does this scholarly work answer the problem or address the topic?
How does this scholarly work neglect to answer the problem or address the topic?

What evidence does the scholarly work present regarding the problem or topic?
What data collection methods were used?
What data analysis methods were used?
What are the strengths of the scholarly work?
What are the limitations of the scholarly work?
What is the theoretical or conceptual framework, if presented?
Does this relate to your study? If so, how?
What are the results of the study?
Include quotes from the scholarly work below (include the page numbers). Use quotes sparingly.
Include the correctly formatted reference here.
Paste the link to the article here.

Comparative Scholarly Works Template

Title of the first journal article:
Title of the second journal article:
What do these articles have in common?
How are the results of these two articles different?
How does this information relate to your proposed study?
Paste the reference and link to the first article here.
Paste the reference and link to the second article here.

Recall that the purpose of the literature review is to provide a synthesis of the existing literature on the problem of practice or topic and to connect the existing literature to the proposed research. Thus, by completing the templates above, you are becoming a scholar on the topic of your research. As you complete these templates over and over using different scholarly works, you should begin to notice information that is repeated. For example, you may notice that the same authors are cited repeatedly. The repetition of authors is information to note since these are possibly the primary scholars in the field related to your topic. Also, identify other repeated information within the scholarly works. For example, if the problem of practice is teacher retention, you may notice words and phrases within many of the articles that are repeated, such as high-stress-levels or low pay. These words may become themes for your literature review. Note repeated words in the *Individual Scholarly Work* template, as you may want to refer back to those particular articles when composing your literature review.

When scholarly works are compared to each other, the similarities and differences between them should become the argument for the purpose of the proposed research. The literature review is NOT simply a summary of the existing literature. Again, the literature review is NOT simply a summary of the existing literature. According to Maxwell (2005),

> The point [of the literature review] is not to *summarize* what has already been done in the field. Instead, it is to ground your proposed study in the relevant previous work, and to give the reader a clear sense of your theoretical approach to the phenomena that you propose to study. (p. 123)

The literature review should present a clear synthesis and analysis of the current literature on the topic of study, and it should present the argument or justification for the proposed research. Additionally, a literature review is not a series of quotes found in the sources; you must use your voice to restate what the authors are saying after you synthesize that information. Again, direct quotes should rarely appear in a quality literature review.

A Strategic Approach to Writing a Literature Review

Below are the basic steps for strategically composing a narrative literature review. Note that there are just a few steps listed, but within each of these steps a lot of work must be accomplished. Also, these steps are presented in a particular order, but in reality, much of the process will overlap. This process is not as much sequential as it is an overlapping process with one step blending into the next step.

General Steps to Compose a Literature Review

1. Determine a specific research question to answer through the literature review. This may be a problem of practice or a specific topic.
2. Locate journal articles and other scholarly sources relevant to the problem or topic.
3. Analyze the information (Individual and Comparative Scholarly Works Templates).
4. Organize and synthesize the information into a justification for the research (Outline).
5. Compose the literature review.

The first step in the literature review process is to determine a problem of practice or topic to address, which was covered in the first chapter. The second step for the literature review is to locate journal articles and scholarly works based on the problem of practice or topic. Once the problem of practice or topic has been established, the analysis process, via the *Individual* and *Comparative Scholarly Works* templates, should commence. After completing a thorough and complete analysis of scholarly works via the templates, organizing the information should be established through drafting and following an outline. Creating an outline for your literature review is a critical step in the process that should not be skipped.

Creating a Literature Review Outline

An outline for a literature review should begin by incorporating the main topics that you determined to be important during your review of the current literature and that must be covered in your written literature review. *Do not skip this step!* When researchers omit this step, they waste a lot of time rewriting work because it is often disorganized and does not make sense. It is difficult to write a literature review that is presented logically without an outline. The outline will serve as a means of guiding your thoughts in a logical manner. It is easier to revise an outline that is presented in an illogical sequence than it is to rewrite an entire literature review that is presented illogically. The main points of the outline will become the main headings for your literature review. Begin with the main topics that you think must be included; then add sub-headings underneath the main headings to further organize your work.

As you read and analyzed the hundreds or thousands of scholarly articles and other sources, you established commonalities and divergent themes via the *Comparative Scholarly Works* template. These themes may become headings for your outline. Categorize the information from the templates into major themes, and those themes may be presented as headings in the literature review. Look for words that were repeated to determine the major headings for your literature review. Within these major themes, you will present the justification for your research. When your literature review is complete, the following information should be established:

- Historical aspects of the problem of practice or topic
- What factors caused the problem of practice or impacted the topic
- How the problem of practice has been solved in the past or how the topic has been addressed in the past
- An argument or justification for the proposed research
- A critical synthesis and analysis of the existing literature
- Well-established presentation of previous research and how the proposed research may advance previous research

- A clear demonstration of the researcher's critical analysis and knowledge about the problem of practice or topic
- A demonstration of how the proposed research may advance current information in the field about the problem of practice or topic
- The theoretical or conceptual framework for your study, if applicable

All the elements above are critical components of a thorough literature review that will establish you as a scholar in the field. An outline will help you to reach this goal. Below is an example of a generic outline for a literature review. Writing a basic outline is a great way to start a literature review. Note that this literature review outline begins with the narrative review. Some literature reviews begin with the narrative review and end with a theoretical framework. Others begin the other way around. Some literature reviews do not include a theoretical framework, and some weave an element of theory throughout the study, when appropriate. Every study will be unique.

Example Literature Review Outline

   I. Overview
  II. Narrative Review (other sub-headings will be added as dictated by your topic)
 III. Summary

This is a very simplistic outline for a literature review, but it establishes a rudimentary idea of how to begin to make an outline for a literature review. Now let's look at how to expand this outline to incorporate the information learned while reading through the hundreds or thousands of scholarly works. The following problem of practice will be utilized to build this outline:

> For this study, the problem is that test scores need to be improved on the Ohio Educational Assessment (OEA) for Science.

The above general outline is expanded below to include the following more specific information as discovered in a review of the literature:

   I. Overview
  II. Narrative Review
    a. Standardized Testing
    b. Characteristics of Standardized Testing
    c. Ohio Educational Assessment for Science
    d. Strategies to Improve Standardized Test Scores
    e. Student Motivation
    f. Teacher Effectiveness
    g. Instructional Resources
    h. Maslow's Hierarchy of Needs
 III. Summary

Note that sub-headings were added to the narrative review section of the outline. As the researcher who is writing the literature review based on the above outline explains each of the headings and makes the argument for the research, the headings will become the guiding factors related to the problem of practice or topic. The last heading added was Maslow's Hierarchy of Needs. This could be appropriate to the study if there are factors that impact student learning that are part of this theory. If the theory was mentioned in multiple scholarly articles, this theory would be applicable. Every study will not have a theoretical component, but if one is mentioned multiple times in the review of the literature for your topic, the theory should be included in your literature review.

As the researcher, you will create an outline similar to the previous example, but your outline will have headings that you discovered to be most relevant to your topic while you are conducting your review of the literature. Each of the headings will be expanded upon as you gather and synthesize more information. The writer of the outline will use the outline to compose a literature review that will guide readers through the information in a logical manner. It is extremely likely that the related literature information will not be presented in a logical order if an outline is not created. Again, this is a very important step that should not be skipped.

Developing a Specific Literature Review Outline

After you have created an outline for your Narrative Review, you will "fill in the blanks." For the previous outline, let's look specifically at the Narrative Review section to determine how it could be organized for a literature review.

I. Overview
II. Narrative Review
  a. Standardized Testing
  b. Characteristics of Standardized Testing
  c. Ohio Educational Assessment for Science
  d. Strategies to Improve Standardized Test Scores
    i. Analysis of data
    ii. Parental involvement
    iii. Bubble students
    iv. Monitoring progress
    v. Instructional practices
  e. Student Motivation
  f. Teacher Effectiveness
    i. Teacher credentials
    ii. Professional development
    iii. New teachers
    iv. Class and school size
    v. Teacher attendance
    vi. Substitute teacher qualifications
  g. Instructional Resources
  h. Maslow's Hierarchy of Needs
III. Summary

For the above outline, the researcher will compose a literature review that is anywhere from 15 to 30 or more pages. As the Narrative Review is written, the writer may discover that additional headings are needed or that perhaps there is not enough information to warrant retaining one or more of the headings. The headings from the outline may be changed as more information is discovered. This is a natural part of the literature review process.

At this point, it may be easy for you to envision how a literature review could become convoluted very quickly without an outline to guide the massive amount of information required. The most effective strategy for writing the literature review is to create a general outline first and then create a more detailed outline as more information is discovered.

More headings could be used in the outline above depending on the information found in the review of the literature, but this outline is an effective representation of an outline that could be used for a literature review. Writing the outline is one of the most important steps for approaching the literature review strategically.

Writing a literature review begins with an understanding of the style that is expected. A literature review is not meant to be poetic and it is not meant to be a novel. A literature review is meant to be scholarly writing. Do not try to impress the audience with unnecessary adjectives. Get to the point and stick to the facts. To quote the famous Dr. Seuss:

So, the writer who breeds more words than he needs, is making a chore for the reader who reads.

Each paragraph of the literature review should begin with a topic sentence. A **topic sentence** introduces the reader to the topic of the paragraph. This may sound elementary, but each paragraph should have a topic sentence that introduces the main point of the paragraph, and every sentence in the paragraph should be directly relevant to the topic of the paragraph. The sentences in each paragraph should develop or expand the main theme or topic of the paragraph. Each paragraph should end with a sentence that transitions to the main point of the next paragraph. This is where the outline will be used as a tool to help you introduce a topic and transition to the next topic, and it will be easy to do if you have an outline to guide you through the process. Without an outline, you are like a ship without a rudder, and will likely end up lost in a sea of confusion and drowning in disorganized information. Note that the last sentence was written in a somewhat poetic fashion. This type of writing should not be included in a literature review.

After your fully developed outline is complete, begin the process of composing the narrative section of the literature review. Remember that, in the narrative section of the literature review, you should present your argument for the proposed research. Review the purposes of the literature review at the beginning of the chapter, and let those purposes guide your choice of words.

Checklist for the Literature Review

☐ The Literature Review begins with an Overview.
☐ The Overview is followed by the Narrative Review.
☐ The Narrative Review presents justification for the rationale for the study.
☐ The Literature Review is not presented as a collection of citations from multiple journal articles.
☐ The Literature Review is presented as a synthesis of the literature.
☐ The Literature Review demonstrates a clear connection between prior research and the proposed research.
☐ The historical context of the problem of practice is clearly presented.
☐ A critical analysis of the literature is evident.
☐ The cause of the problem, as identified in the literature, is presented (if known).
☐ Prior solutions are presented.
☐ Solutions to the problem found in the literature are presented.
☐ Most journal articles (approximately 80%) are less than five years since publication.
☐ The Literature Review is focused on solving the problem.
☐ The authors' voice is heard throughout the literature review.
☐ Each paragraph begins with a topic sentence.
☐ The Literature Review is written concisely.

Conclusion

In this chapter, the importance of writing an outline for a literature review was stressed. The narrative and possible theoretical elements of a literature review were explained in detail. The process of writing a literature review begins by locating relevant scholarly works. A thorough analysis and comparison of scholarly works must follow. The comparison of scholarly works is followed up with the development of a general and specific outline to guide and organize the literature review. The outline is then developed into the argument for the proposed research in the narrative section of the literature review.

Chapter Highlights

According to the American Psychological Association (APA, 2020), the peer-review process is defined as the process when a potential journal article manuscript is reviewed and evaluated by the authors' peers in the scientific community based on the quality and potential contribution of each article. Peer-reviewed articles in the literature review should represent the latest findings about a proposed problem of practice or research topic.

The literature review section of an educational report will generally be 15 to 30 pages long (if not longer).

A literature review for an educational report may or may not have a specific theoretical framework.

The Overview is the first section of the literature review section, and it introduces the reader to the broad topics addressed in the review of the literature. This section should be relatively brief and should mention the problem and purpose of the study followed by the topics of the literature review.

The literature review presents the justification or argument for the problem of practice or research topic. It should help the researcher determine possible solutions or recommendations for the problem of the research.

Purposes of the literature review include: (1) disclosing historical aspects of the problem of practice or topic, (2) detailing factors that may impact the problem or topic, (3) conveying an argument for conducting the proposed research, (4) presenting critical and analyses of existing literature, (5) establishing the state of previous research and how the proposed research will advance the topic, and (6) demonstrating the researcher's knowledge and ability to critically analyze a problem, practice, or topic.

A primary source is "a publication written by the individual or individuals who actually conducted the work presented in the publication" (Gall et al., 1996, p. 54).

A secondary source is "a publication in which the author reviews research studies, theories, and educational practices and programs that others have generated about that particular problem or topic" (Gall et al., 1996, p. 54).

The vast majority of the information in the literature review should come from primary sources, and all information must be cited.

Rudestam and Newtons (2007) noted several important aspects of writing that are important to remember to compose a quality literature review: (1) be a convincing writer; (2) be a critic, not a reporter; (3) be a selective writer; (4) be a skillful researcher; and (5) be a reasonable problem solver.

A well-written literature review reflects data collection, analysis, interpretation, and conclusions that are beneficial beyond the current study. The quality of the literature review establishes the author's credibility as a researcher, thus the presentation, organization, and inclusion and exclusion of information, must be intentional and must be scholarly.

Reviewing literature involves searching, browsing, skimming, reading, saving, and organizing scholarly works that are relevant to the proposed problem of practice or topic. The internet is the fastest and most effective way to locate scholarly sources. If you are enrolled as a student or work for a college or university, it is likely that you have free access to excellent sources of scholarly works through sources such as Ebsco Host and ProQuest.

Other ways of searching for scholarly sources include Google Scholar, ERIC, Oxford Reference Online, and Britannica Online.

Many library databases give you the option to limit your search results to include only peer-reviewed articles, which is a very helpful tool for locating scholarly, peer-reviewed journal articles.

Wikipedia is a good source for learning a quick tidbit of information, but for the purposes of scholarly writing, Wikipedia information should be verified by a true scholarly source.

Organizing information is a critical component of writing an effective literature review. From the very beginning of a search for scholarly sources, the researcher should establish a system that works for him or her to organize the scholarly articles that are reviewed. There many ways to do this, and researchers needs to determine the method that works best for themselves.

Composing a literature review begins with a system or a plan for incorporating the vast amount of information that has been read and organized. Formulating and writing an outline effectively is likely the best way to begin writing the literature review. An outline helps ensure the literature review is well-organized and that the writers' thoughts flow smoothly. As new information is gathered and synthesized, the outline will need to be revised, but doing this ensures an effective literature review develops.

When the literature review is complete, the following information should be established:

- Historical aspects of the problem of practice or topic
- What factors caused the problem of practice or impacted the topic
- How the problem of practice has been solved in the past or how the topic has been addressed in the past
- An argument or justification for the proposed research
- A critical synthesis and analysis of the existing literature
- Well-established presentation of previous research and how the proposed research may advance previous research
- A clear demonstration of the researcher's critical analysis and knowledge about the problem of practice or topic
- A demonstration of how the proposed research may advance current information in the field about the problem of practice or topic
- The theoretical or conceptual framework for your study, if applicable

Interviews and Focus Groups

Objectives

By the end of this chapter, the reader will be able to:

- Differentiate between interviews and focus groups
- Explain the different types of interviews
- Write appropriate interview questions
- Differentiate between types of questions
- Identify pitfalls to avoid when writing interview and survey questions
- State the procedures for conducting interviews
- Describe the process for writing the interviews procedures and findings sections of an educational report
- Explain transcribing, script dialog, and coding in relation to an educational report

Key Terms

- Coding
- Interview
- Focus group
- Grounded in the literature
- Open-ended questions
- Purposeful sampling
- Sampling

- Script dialog
- Semi-structured interview
- Snowball sampling
- Structured interview
- Themes
- Transcribing
- Unstructured interview

Introduction

Two popular approaches used to gather information are interviews and focus groups. Both approaches involve real-time conversations with the participants. Interviews and focus groups can elicit rich and deep information where other data collection methods may fall short. When choosing between an interview or focus group, you must assess the pros and cons of each approach before collecting data. However, the procedures and analysis used for interviews and focus groups are very similar. For this reason, this chapter will concentrate on interviews with the understanding that, with a few modifications, these techniques can be applied to focus groups. In this chapter, you will learn about the differences between interviews and focus groups, types of interviews, writing interview questions, the steps required to conduct interviews, and writing the data collection procedures and findings sections of your educational report.

Differences between Interviews and Focus Groups

Interviews and focus groups are both qualitative data techniques that can provide rich and deep information regarding the problem of practice. An **interview** is a conversation between an interviewer and interviewee. The interviewer asks the questions and the interviewee responds to the questions. This form of person-to-person communication provides more personal information regarding an event or situation. Similar to the interview, is the focus group.

A **focus group** is a form of person-to-group communication, and it is also a way of collecting rich and detailed information; however, focus groups tend to be less personal. The focus group usually consists of five to eight participants. The interviewer asks questions and the focus group members respond to the questions. The focus group is a more efficient and cost-effective way to collect information in that it allows participants to springboard off each other's answers and trigger new trains of thoughts. However, because some people may feel intimidated in a group setting, the focus group may cause some participants to be less likely to share their true feelings and opinions; this makes focus groups less personal as compared to interviews.

Understanding Various Types of Interviews

Interviews can be either structured, unstructured, or semi-structured. Most researchers use semi-structured interviews in applied research; however, the other types of interviews may be used. Each type has its advantages and disadvantages. When answering the central research question, you must choose the interview approach that best addresses the goals of the study. Below are the three type of interviews:

Structured Interview: The **structured interview** is a formal data collection method that employs a series of pre-set interview questions. The interviewer reads the questions to each participant exactly as they are written and in the exact same order and with no variation. By maintaining structure and order, you can easily compare answers across different interviewees, which, in turn, increases the reliability of the data. However, structured interviews require a lot of expertise and preparation to develop the questions. A complete review of related literature on the research topic should be done before composing the interview questions. The structured interview is best used when the researcher is interested in gathering opinions or information quickly and efficiently among a large group of individuals. Structured interviews provide more breadth than depth and are not recommended when trying to dig deeply into a situation or issue.

Unstructured Interview: The **unstructured interview** is best described as an informal conversation or chat. The interview is topic-driven and requires little preparation. Unlike a structured interview, the unstructured interview does not rely on preset questions. Instead, the interviewer engages the interviewee on a particular topic in a relaxed, carefree conversational style. The unstructured interview is best used when the researcher is interested in exploring a new situation or issue that has never been addressed. By eliminating the structured questions, interviewees may be more willing to freely share their opinions without the bias or confinement associated with structured questions. To begin an unstructured interview, the researcher just asks a general question related to the topic, then the researcher lets the conversation develop naturally. A disadvantage to the unstructured interview is sometimes the interviewee gets off topic and begins to ramble. This may prove to be time-consuming when the researcher has to transcribe interviews and sort through the data. Unstructured interviews are usually avoided or rarely used in applied research.

Semi-Structured Interview: The **semi-structured interview** is best described as a combination of the structured and unstructured interviews. Borrowing the best elements from both types of approaches, the semi-structured interview begins by relying on preset questions, yet, during the interview process, the interviewer has the freedom to follow up with unstructured questions that may seek clarification. The semi-structured interview is best used when the researcher is interested in exploring a situation with depth while maintaining order and increased reliability of the data. Just like the structured interview, a complete review of related literature on the topic should be done before composing the interview questions. Semi-structured interviews are the most popular approach used in applied research.

Writing Interview Questions

When developing interview questions, you should skillfully compose the interview questions with the goal of answering the central question of the study. Developing quality interview questions can take time, and you should contemplate and refine each question until it is just right. Below are tips to help you write quality interview questions.

Ground the questions in the literature: Before constructing interview questions, you must complete a thorough and complete review of the literature. In general, it is recommended that researchers read at least a few hundred peer-reviewed journal articles to become vastly familiar with the evidence presented in the literature. The questions should be **grounded in the literature** meaning that the researcher has conducted a thorough investigation of the current literature related to the research problem. The interview questions must be generated from the most current related research (published within the past five years). Each interview question needs to be supported with at least one citation to denote the source from which the survey question is grounded, though multiple citations are ideal and recommended. Below is an example of an interview question considered well-grounded in the literature.

How does socioeconomic status affect student OEA scores at your school?

"A review of the literature revealed that, in many schools, socioeconomic status seemed to impact test scores (Von Stumm & Plomin, 2015). Thus, this question was developed to determine whether the participants believed that socioeconomic status was a factor in the OEA scores at this specific school."

This is an appropriate interview question because the researcher discovered, during the review of the current literature, that one possible factor that may impact OEA scores is socioeconomic status.

Use open-ended questions: Interview questions are usually in the form of open-ended questions. Good **open-ended** questions require the interviewee to contemplate the questions being asked and then provide thoughtful explanations of their answers. Participants have the opportunity to elaborate on the questions or prompts in their own words. Open-ended questions require more time and effort to complete and are reserved for face-to-face interviews in applied research. This is in stark contrast to closed-ended questions with fixed answers that require simple, predetermined responses such as a "yes" or "no" answer. Open-ended questions often begin with "What," "How," or "Why." Below are examples:

What is your opinion on the cause of low parental involvement at your school?

How would you describe student behavior during recess?

Why do you believe school should be year-round?

Notice that the participant is asked to elaborate on, in his or her own words, the questions.

Tips for Writing Interview Questions

The outcome of a good interview is directly related to the information and expertise that goes into developing the interview questions. Interview questions need to be created to elicit the information that is needed to help guide you to formulate a solution to the problem of practice being studied. Below are some pitfalls to avoid when creating survey questions.

Avoid Leading Questions: A leading question subtly influences the interviewee to answer a certain way by assuming a particular experience, situation, or outcome that may or may not be true. For example, the first question below is a poor question because the word "unpleasant" implies that the interviewee's high school experience was somehow bad. This may or may not be true. The better question removes the bias and makes the question neutral.

Poor Question: *How unpleasant was your high school experience?*

Better Question: *How would you describe your high school experience?*

Avoid Loaded Questions: A loaded question implies that the interviewee engaged in an activity or attended a situation that is controversial, unjust, or illegal. For example, the first question below is a poor question because it assumes the interviewee engages in an illegal activity. This type of question may discourage the interviewee from continuing in the survey. A better question would use a qualifying question; by doing so, you will provide the interviewee the opportunity to dispute the claim.

Poor Question: *How do illegal drugs affect your schoolwork?*

Better Question (with qualifier): *Do you use illegal drugs? If so, how do illegal drugs affect your schoolwork?*

Avoid Push Questions: The push question tricks the interviewee into answering the question in a certain way. Unlike a leading question, the interviewer is aware of the implication of the question and purposely tries to get an answer to support their claim. For example, the first question below is a poor question because it forces the interviewee to agree with the interviewer's presupposition that the "superintendent is a dysfunctional manager." This type of question is unethical. The better question removes any innuendos or opinions and makes the question neutral.

Poor Question: *Rumor has it that your superintendent is a dysfunctional manager; how would you describe his leadership style?*

Better Question: *How would you describe your superintendence's leadership style?*

Avoid Double-Barreled Questions: The double-barreled question touches on two or more subjects within the same question. For example, the first question given is a poor question because it asked the interviewee to describe both breakfast and lunch at the same time. This type of question may confuse the answer because the interviewee may have completely different opinions regarding each dining experience. A better question would be to use two separate questions.

Poor Question: *How would you describe the cafeteria's food during breakfast and lunch?*

Better Question: *How would you describe the cafeteria's food during breakfast?*

Better Question: *How would you describe the cafeteria's food during lunch?*

Avoid Absolute Questions: The absolute question contains absolute terms such as "all," "never," "always," "everybody," "no one," "only," etc. and focuses the interviewee's attention on unrealistic events or situations. For example, the first question below is a poor question because it asks the interviewee to assume a group of students is "always" late to class. The interviewee may disagree with the absoluteness of the questions, discrediting it as an extreme case, and in turn may cause uncertainty in the interviewee's replies. A better question is one that is written to avoid absolutes.

Poor Question: *What can be done about students who are always late to class?*

Better Question: *What can be done about students who are late to class?*

Avoid Poorly Worded Questions: A confusing or poorly worded question uses words that are unclear and/or inappropriate for a particular audience. The interviewer uses the words that are not within the participant's vocabulary or are poor word choices. For example, the first question below is a poorly worded question because it uses the word "delineate." The interviewee may be unaware of the meaning of the word. A better question would use a simpler word (describe).

Poor Question: *How would you delineate your college experience?*

Better Question: *How would you describe your college experience?*

Avoid Long Questions: A long question may cause the participants to get tired or bored. You should use short sentences. For example, the first question below is a poorly worded question because it is wordy. A better question would be a shorter and more concise sentence.

Poor Question: *Because of the tremendous increase in computer use among students and the rise in artificial intelligence, how do you feel about artificial intelligence being used in the classroom?*

Better Question: *How do you feel about artificial intelligence being used in the classroom?*

Conducting the Interviews

Interview data collection should follow established protocol and be conducted synchronously: face-to-face, phone call, or e-conference. However, an unconventional form of interview may take place via an internet chat room as long as the interview is in a "real time" environment. Regardless of the medium used to conduct the interview, all interview procedures must consist of specific elements.

Step 1. Ensure accessibility: Accessibility is the ability of participants to be easily reached. Lack of access to personnel who may have key information to solving the problem of practice may result in inadequate solutions. For example, if high school students are needed to be interviewed, but school is closed for the summer, accessibility may not be possible until the following school year. For this reason, you should consider accessibility before beginning the research.

Step 2. Get permission to conduct the research: Permission is the act of securing approval or authorization to conduct the research from the organization being studied. This is often referred to as site approval and should be provided in writing. While seeking permission, the leadership and/or stakeholders at the site should be informed regarding the nature of the study, personnel who will be involved in the study, length of the study, and what will be done with the information. Approval to conduct research must come from a person with appropriate site authority and should be obtained in writing. Some organizations may require Institutional Review Board (IRB) approval before conducting the research, however, if the applied research is site-specific, solutions to the problem are not generalizable, and the project will not be published or disseminated beyond the site, it most likely will not require IRB approval.

Step 3. Identify your participants for the interview: This may seem logical, but it is often tempting to solicit participants who are easily accessible and convenient for your study, but who are not a good fit for the study. Also, do not fall into the temptation to solicit participants who simply agree with you or you are too close to. For example, if you are a third-grade teacher with a grievance toward teachers in the second grade that you feel do not adequately prepare students for third grade, it would not be wise to choose to interview only third grade teachers who agree with your point-of-view regarding second grade teachers. There may be two problems with this study. One: you may be too close to the research to remain unbiased. And two: both second and third grade teachers would need to have a voice to help solve the problem. Choosing logical participants means that you will gain the most relevant information from the participants chosen to help solve the problem of practice. Again, convenience is not necessarily the most logical choice for soliciting participants.

Step 4. Select sampling procedures: Sampling is the process of selecting people or things from a representative population. Two of the most common sampling procedures used for interviews are purposeful sampling and snowball sampling. **Purposeful sampling** means that the researcher selects individuals as participants because they can purposefully inform an understanding of the research problem or topic (Creswell, 2013). Purposeful sampling helps to ensure the selected participants are information-rich (Patton, 2002), which may lend to solving the problem of practice. It is arguably the most utilized form of sampling in applied research. Purposeful sampling relies on the researcher's reasonable judgment and expertise for selecting participants. Before selecting participants to be interviewed, you must consider the goals of your study and how to reach those goals. For this reason, applied research often uses purposeful sampling when selecting interviewees, and you must have a purpose or good reason for selecting the participants. It is often wise to clearly state why the participants were chosen and justify their usefulness to solving the problem. **Snowball sampling** means that participants are recommended by other people or participants who know additional individuals who may offer information-rich data to help solve the problem of practice (Gall et al., 2006). For example, if you are researching the lack of female administrators in a particular school district, one administrator participant in your study may be able to put you in contact with a few other female administrators who are either currently administrators or are seeking to become administrators and who may be willing to serve as participants for the study.

Step 5. Secure logistics: Logistics are the requirements that pertain to managing people, securing facilities, and obtaining supplies. Before conducting an interview, ensure that all logistical requirements are addressed. Logistics are best discussed in terms of when and where will the data be collected, from whom will the data be collected, how will the data be collected, how will the data be recorded, etc. If you are conducting a phone call or e-conference, make sure you have a clear connection. If conducting face-to-face interviews, make sure the facility where you will be conducting them is comfortable and free from distraction.

Step 6. Record the interview: Ensure your method for recording data is properly working and the sound quality is appropriate. A clear recording will help you with transcription during data analysis. You are also encouraged to take notes during interviews; this will help you reflect on answers, highlight important themes, and retain information.

Step 7. Include opening statements: Begin interviews by introducing yourself. Inform the interviewee of the purpose of the study and why the study is important. Provide instructions on how you will conduct the interview and its format. Address any issues pertaining to confidentiality, and then ask the interviewee if they are comfortable participating in the study and/or have any questions.

Step 8. Collect demographic information: Immediately following the opening statement is a great time to collect demographic information. It is important to collect demographic information when conducting research to identify groups of people who behave or respond in similar ways. Demographic information common to most research is age, sex, and ethnicity. For applied research, other demographic information may be needed, such as the participant's job title, type of education, years of experience, grade level, socio-economic status, etc. Remember, only collect demographic information that is relevant to your study and no more. Finally, use pseudonyms when describing individuals who have participated in interviews. Pseudonyms should be presented using the appropriate title of the participant such as principal, teacher, parent, legal guardian, student, etc. For example, if you interview one administrator and four teachers, then your participant pseudonyms would be *Administrator One, Teacher One, Teacher Two, Teacher Three,* and *Teacher Four.* Using pseudonyms helps preserve the privacy and confidentiality of the participants in case there is a breach in the data.

Step 9. Ask the interview questions: Make sure you have your questions established before the interview. It is good practice to use the same open-ended questions for all interviewees. Doing this makes your data easier to interpret, analyze, and compare. Conduct yourself in a professional manner and always be aware of your tone of voice, facial expressions, and body language, all of which may inadvertently bias the interviewees answers.

Step 10. Include closing statements: Before closing the interview, ask the interviewee if they have any questions or if he/she has any additional information to add. Remind the interviewee that their participation in the interview will be beneficial to addressing the problem of practice. Close the interview by thanking the participant.

 Go to *www.khlearn.com* to watch a video about conducting interviews and focus groups.

Writing the Interviews Procedures

The procedures section for applied research may contain multiple approaches. For that reason, begin the procedures section of the educational report with an overview of the section. The Overview should begin with a brief restatement of the nature and purpose of the study in relationship to the educational site. Following the relationship to the site, the different analyses that will be used will be presented. The Procedure Section should be organized by approach. The approach we will focus on in this section is interviews.

See Procedures Overview example below:

PROCEDURES

Overview

The purpose of this study was to provide recommendations to the leadership team at Hampton High School with possible solutions to the problem of students' low test scores on the Ohio Educational Assessment (OEA) for Science. Hampton High School is a mid-size suburban public high school in southeastern Ohio. This portion of the report provides interview procedures, survey procedures, and documents procedures.

Writing the Interviews Procedures

The procedures section for applied research is a step-by-step process that is presented in narrative form. When using interviews as an approach, you should include the various elements of the interviews in your write-up. Begin by describing the type of interview you will use (e.g., semi-structure, structured, or unstructured). Next, describe the persons you plan to interview and the sampling techniques that will be used to elicit participants. When describing the people you plan to interview, be general in describing their positions, and then justify why they are the best persons for addressing the problem of practice.

See Interviews Procedures example below:

Interviews Procedures

The first approach used to collect data in this study was semi-structured interviews. This approach allowed the researcher to construct interview questions based on specific topics to be investigated, and it allowed the researcher to format questions in a way that incorporated previous answers based on each participant's experiences. Conducting interviews allowed the researcher to determine how teachers and administrators would solve the problem of low scores on the Ohio Educational Assessment (OEA) for Science at Hampton High School located in southeastern Ohio. Purposeful sampling was used to elicit participants (Bickman & Rog, 2009). The five faculty members consisted of one administrator, two 9th grade teachers, and three 11th grade teachers. The participants were selected based on their historical familiarity with the OEA for Science and the assessment results for Hampton High School.

Once that is completed, describe in detail how and where you plan to conduct the interviews. Interview data collection should follow established protocol and should be conducted synchronously: face-to-face, phone call, or e-conference. However, an unconventional form of interview may take place (such as via an internet chat room) as long as the interview is in a "real time" environment. See the example below.

The interviews were conducted off-campus in a one-on-one, face-to-face format. Standard interview protocol was utilized during the interviews (Creswell, 2015). Each interview lasted approximately one hour and was recorded and immediately transcribed for data analysis. Throughout the interview, the researcher made note of body language and tone during the interviews to further define the participants' thoughts and feelings toward each topic included in the interview. After participants consented to participate in the study, the 16 questions below were utilized for the interviews.

Now include how you will analyze the data. Discuss transcribing, coding, and theme development. See the example below.

Once interviews were transcribed, the transcripts were reviewed, and coding was used to determine the categories and themes present in the participants' dialogue. Coding and categorization were appropriate data analysis methods as they allowed the researcher to align the participants' responses with the literature related to the study (Creswell & Poth, 2018). This data analysis method also lends itself to the creation of a table of codes, from which the researcher determined what constitutes an entry under a specific theme along with what does not (Creswell & Poth, 2018). Generally speaking, coding involves reading the transcript from each interview and identifying the various themes that are represented throughout. To answer the central research question, data were collected in a qualitative manner via 16 semi-structured questions. After participants consented to participate in the study, the following 16 questions were utilized for the interviews.

Conclude the interview procedures with your interview questions. Each interview question should be stated and then justified and supported by the literature. Some questions may be "incidental" or not supported by the literature; however, a rational reason must still be given for including those questions.
See Interview Questions example below:

Interview Questions

1. What skills are assessed with the OEA for Science?

This question aimed to determine educators' awareness of how the OEA for Science is aligned with Next Generation Science Standards (NGSS). Understanding the alignment of an assessment with standards in terms of rigor and content is critical to ensuring the assessment accurately measures students' abilities with the material and skills (Carnegie Mellon University, 2019). By asking this question, the researcher will learn how familiar teachers are with which skills and concepts are assessed on the OEA.

2. How are these skills incorporated through students' 9-12 curriculum map?

This question aimed to determine educators' familiarity with the standards included on the OEA for Science and how they are incorporated into the science course offerings at Hampton High School. Ensuring that all concepts to be assessed are taught at an appropriate rigor level throughout the courses that all students are required to take is necessary to provide students the academic experiences necessary to be successful on the test (Drake & Burns, 2004). Likewise, understanding the vertical alignment of science course offerings at Hampton High School may create a cohesive experience for students prior to taking the assessment (Case, 2005).

Checklist for the Interview Procedures

- ☐ Does the Interview Procedures include the type of interview (structures, unstructured, semi-structured) and its justification (including a citation)?
- ☐ Does the Interview Procedures include sampling type (purposeful sampling, snowball, etc.)?
- ☐ Does the Interview Procedures identify the participants?
- ☐ Does the Interview Procedures identify the rationale for participant selection?
- ☐ Does the Interview Procedures include how the interviews were conducted (face-to-face, phone, etc.)?
- ☐ Does the Interview Procedures briefly explain data analysis procedures?
- ☐ Does the Interview Procedures include the number of interview questions?
- ☐ Does the Interview Procedures include the interview questions and their rationale (the majority of questions should be cited using the literature)?
- ☐ The Interview Procedures is written in paragraph format.
- ☐ The Interview Procedures is written in past tense.

Analyzing the Interviews Data

After the interviews are completed, you are ready to analyze the data. The data should contain rich and detailed information regarding the problem you want to solve. You will now need to search through the data and start finding themes. Themes are common perceptions or patterns of information provided by the interviewees that address the goals of the study. To find themes, you should consider the following established procedures for analyzing the data. Begin by collecting all your notes, documents, recordings, etc. and sorting them into a well-organized system for easy retrieval and analysis. Consider placing the data in files and folders that are labeled with brief descriptions of the content, date, time, location, and names of interviewees. Make backup copies and file audio recordings and digital media for safe keeping.

Transcribing

After organizing the data for easy retrieval, it is time to transcribe your interviews. **Transcribing** is the process of putting human speech into written form. This can be done by listening to the recorded interview then typing each and every word (sound, expression, etc.) into a word processing document. The transcript should be in a script dialog format. **Script dialog** is similar to the dialog between characters in a movie script or screen play. Put a space between each speaker's comments as they go back and forth in a conversational style. If adding clarity to the conversation, you should use brackets as you are deviating from the original source. After the transcript is completed, you should double check the transcript by replaying the audio recording while reading the transcript to ensure the dialog is accurately written. At the beginning of your transcript, always include the name of the interviewer and interviewee, date and time of the interview, and location of where the interview took place.

See Interview Template below:

Interview Template

General Information Questions	
Participants' Name	Mrs. Smith
Date/Time	November 14, 2019, 2:00 PM
Site	Brookfield Elementary School
Method	Face-to-Face
Participant Demographics	
Current Age	39
Gender	Female
Race/Ethnicity	Caucasian, Non-Hispanic
Occupation	Ninth grade teacher
Interview Questions	

Interviewer: What skills are assessed on the Ohio Educational Assessment for Science?
Interviewee: Well. I haven't seen the OEA, but I would assume that they would assess skills like data analysis and interpretation of data and things like that like you would expect in science. [Note: look of concern on interviewee's face].
Interviewer: How are these skills incorporated throughout the curricula?
Interviewee: Well, in the past, students have learned things through our learning goals which are all supposed to be associated with a specific science skill that we want them to learn, so those are kind of interwoven in our learning goals. And we've done a little separation of that to make assessment of content a little bit easier. The scientific practices have to be part of the actual assessment, especially for the lower level kids, but I think most of the teachers in the department when we hire them, we try to hire teachers that really believe in doing science. And I think we've been pretty successful with that.
Continue with transcribing the interview...

Once all the interviews have been transcribed, it is time to identify themes within the data; this is done using coding. **Coding** is a systematic process of identifying key passages and text, then making relationships between the words, phrases, and concepts. Coding is a hands-on process that may require the use of note taking, mark-up, highlighting, and note cards. When coding, keep in mind that you are a "human interpreter" of the data, so trust your judgment and intuition. Following are instructions on how to systematically identify codes from transcripts.

Coding the Data

To code your data, begin by reading and re-reading the transcripts numerous times to become intimate with the data. Each time you read through the manuscript, make notes in the margins. Look for reoccurring key words, beliefs, and opinions, and anything that stands out. Trust your judgment and intuition and make note of anything that catches your attention when making notes. Review the notes you made in the margin and identify keywords, phrases, and concepts. Mentally organize the notes into categories, and then, using a set of colored markers, assign a different color marker to each keyword. For example:

Blue marker = Assessment

Yellow marker = Instruction

Orange marker = Resources

Purple marker = Literacy

Green = Staffing

Re-read the entire transcripts and underline the text with different color markers associated with the keywords; by doing so, you will begin to uncover common themes. Once you have critically reviewed and coded the data, begin to identify patterns by comparing the interviews. The patterns you identify will emerge as themes. **Themes** are prominent ideas that surface from the transcriptions. Themes should be specified and related directly to the research questions. Use a *Codes and Themes* table to help further develop your themes. Support your themes by using direct quotes gathered from the transcripts. For example, in the *Codes and Themes* table include "Assessment," note how the theme "Assessment" emerged using direct quotes from the interviewees to support the theme. See Table 1 *Codes and Themes* table.

Table 1: *Codes and Themes from the Interview Data*

Themes	Codes	Examples of Participants' Words
Data Analysis	Data	Systems should be in place within the district to secure individual results, aggregate and generalize performance to identify strengths and weaknesses.
	Item analysis	I think it would be interesting to look at the distribution of questions on the OEA and how we're covering those things in curriculum and in what years we're doing it.
	Interpretation	I was confused on how to interpret the assessment data. It would be nice to be able to meet with other professionals on how to interpret this data.
Collaboration	Working Together	Grade 11 teachers have been provided with the bank of released questions and scoring guides published by the Ohio DOE, but all teachers use the information independently. It would be beneficial if we could collaborate on this together.
	Community	Creating a positive learning community may encourage our students and teachers to work together forming a science club or science fair.
	Team work	There has been discussion about maybe using a team approach to help those lowest achieving students to be pulled up a little bit. This would include the special education teachers and other resources.
	Sharing with others	When teachers share their resources, students benefit.
Professional Development	Teacher learning	There's never been any special effort put into teacher learning regarding the OEAs for Science as far as I'm aware in my tenure in the department.

Themes	Codes	Examples of Participants' Words
	In-service	Most teachers seem to want more in-service training session so that they are better trained to support students on the OEA. If teachers were specifically trained on how to support students for the assessment, it is likely that scores could improve.
	Teacher training	Teachers need ongoing support and training in order to help increase scores on the assessment. To my knowledge, there has never been a training session for teachers.
	Certification	It would be nice if teachers could receive some sort of certification before administering the assessment. This may seem far-fetched, but I would imagine that it would help to increase scores.

Now, using the themes and coded words identified, search and find how many times the words appear in the transcripts by using the (search/find command) in your computer's word processer. Use a Frequency of Codes table to help further support your themes. For example, the Frequency of Codes table below includes "Collaboration." Note how the theme "Collaboration" appears 15 times throughout the transcripts. See Table 2 for Frequency of Codes table.

Table 2: *Frequency of Codes across Interview Data*

Themes	Code Word	Occurrences Across Data
Data Analysis	Analysis	9
	Assessments	4
	Data Interpretation	7
Collaboration	Working together	5
	Community	5
	Team work	2
	Sharing with others	3
Professional Development	Teacher learning	4
	In-service	3
	Teacher training	6
	Certification	7

Writing the Interviews Findings

The Findings Section for applied research may contain multiple analyses. For that reason, begin the findings section of the educational report with an overview of the section. The Overview should begin with a brief restatement of the nature and purpose of the study in relationship to the educational site. Following the relationship to the site, the different analyses that will be used will be presented. The Findings Section should be organized by approach.

See Findings Overview example below:

FINDINGS

Overview

The purpose of this study was to provide recommendations to the leadership team at Hampton High School with possible solutions to the problem of low test scores on the Ohio Educational Assessment (OEA) for Science. This section of the report includes interview findings, survey findings, and documents findings.

The Interviews Findings Write-Up

Begin writing the Interviews Findings section by describing the type of interview used (e.g., semi-structure, structured, or unstructured) and the purpose for conducting the interviews. Include how and where the interviews were conducted. Next, describe the number of participants and the persons you interviewed. Conclude with a brief description of the interview process.

See Interview Findings example below:

Interview Findings

The first approach used in this study was interviews. Semi-structured interviews consisting of 16 questions were conducted with each participant on an individual basis. The purpose of these interviews was to focus on the factors that impact the low test scores on the Ohio Educational Assessment (OEA) for Science at Hampton High School. Interviews were conducted off-site, either at the local public library or at a restaurant. A total of five participants took part in the fact-to-face interviews. The participant criteria for interviews were a tenure of 3 years or more at Hampton High School and a familiarity with the OEA for Science. Because of their tenure at the school, these participants have been directly involved in science instruction, analysis of the OEA scores, or both. Prior to beginning each interview, participants were provided with a brief summary of the purpose of the study in addition to the information they received when invited to participate in the study. Each interview lasted approximately 1 hour and were recorded and immediately transcribed for data analysis. Throughout the interview, the researcher made note of body language and tone demonstrated during the interviews to further define the participants' thoughts and feelings toward each topic included in the interview.

Next, each participant should then be described separately using one paragraph per participant. Describe the participants with a focus on their positions, experience, and expertise related to the problem.

See Interview Description of Participants example below:

Interview Descriptions of Participants

The first interview candidate was Mrs. Harrison, the building principal, with 29 years of experience in education, eight of which were spent as an administrator at Hampton High School. Prior to entering administration, she was an elementary teacher, teaching both math and English, and her administrative experience started at the middle school level. Because of her experiences at all three levels of education, Mrs. Harrison brought a unique and interesting perspective to the study.

Mr. Gilmer is currently in his second year as a co-department chair and has been teaching at Hampton High School for 15 years, with 3 years as a teacher elsewhere prior. While he teaches mostly 12th grade students who have already taken the Ohio Educational Assessment (OEA) for Science prior to enrolling in his course, Mr. Gilmer's leadership within the science department, as well as his keen eye for data analysis, has resulted in a strong familiarity with the OEA for Science and its results at Hampton High School, along with experience discussing these results with others.

Mrs. Smith is the other co-department chair and has been a science teacher for 13 years, all of which have been spent at Hampton High School. Historically, Mrs. Smith has taught 9th grade science and biology, both of which are courses that students enroll in prior to their junior year, during which they take the OEA for Science.

After describing the interviewees, share the codes, themes, and supporting quotations from participants. *See example Codes and Themes from the Interview Data below.*

Table 1. Codes and Themes from the Interview Data

Themes	Codes	Examples of Participants' Words
Data Analysis	Data	Systems should be in place within the district to mine individual results, aggregate and generalize performance to identify strengths and weaknesses.
	Item analysis	I think it would be interesting to look at the distribution of questions on the OEA and how we're covering those things in curriculum and in what years we're doing it.
	Interpretation	I was confused on how to interpret the assessment data. It would be nice to be able to meet with other professionals on how to interpret this data.
Collaboration	Working together	Grade 11 teachers have been provided with the bank of released questions and scoring guides published by the Ohio DOE, but all teachers use the information independently. It would be beneficial if we could collaborate on this together
	Community	Creating a positive learning community may encourage our students and teachers to work together forming a science club or science fair.
	Team work	There has been discussion about maybe using a

End with a frequency of codes across the interview data. Search for key words using the search/find command in your word processor then create a table.

See the Themes and Frequency Codes Across Interview Data table below.

Table 2. Themes and Frequency Codes Across Interview Data

Themes	Code Word	Occurrences Across Data
Data Analysis	Analysis	9
	Assessments	4
	Data interpretation	7
Collaboration	Working together	5
	Community	5
	Team work	2
	Sharing with others	3
Professional Development	Teacher learning	4
	In-service	3
	Teacher training	6
	Certification	7

Finally, end with a discussion of the findings and any takeaways that emerged from the interviews. Use direct quotes, when appropriate, to support takeaways in the discussion section.

See Interview Discussion of the Findings example below:

Interview Discussion of the Findings

Three overarching themes developed from the interviews. The first was data analysis, the second theme was collaboration, and the third theme was professional development.

Data Analysis. The first theme that was evident was analyzing data. For example, a participant stated, "I was confused on how to interpret the assessment data. It would be nice to be able to meet with other professionals on how to interpret this data." Several participants reported that there is limited time allotted for data analysis among teachers, but that a desire to conduct such analysis exists. Data interpretation seems to be the most difficult aspect of data analysis. Data interpretation was mentioned seven times (see table 2 above) in the interviews as most participants seemed to struggle with understanding the data and applying it to their teaching.

Collaboration. The second theme that was evident was collaboration as numerous teachers expressed an interest in working with fellow teachers. According to one participant, "Grade 11 teachers have been provided with the bank of released questions and scoring guides published by the Ohio DOE, but all teachers use the information independently. It would be beneficial if we could collaborate on this together." Further, teachers desired to work together and felt a sense of community. Both "working together" and "community" were mentioned five times by participants, which reiterated the importance of collaboration. One participant stated, "Creating a positive learning community may encourage our students and teachers to work together forming a science club or science fair." Most participants expressed a desire to share resources with one another and work together to help increase scores on the OEA.

Professional Development. The third theme that was evident was professional development. Professional development was mentioned a total of 20 times in the

Checklist for the Interview Findings

☐ Does the Interview Findings include the type of interview?
☐ Does the Interview Findings include a brief overview of the procedures?
☐ Does the Interview Findings include a Description of Participants?
☐ Does the Interview Findings include Interview Results in the form of tables to include coding, quotations, and frequency word counts?
☐ Does the Interview Findings include a discussion of the findings and interpretation?
☐ Does the Interview Findings include a discussion of themes with supporting evidence?
☐ The Interview Findings is written in paragraph format.
☐ The Interview Findings is written in past tense.

Conclusion

Chapter 5 began with an introduction to the procedures for conducting interviews and focus groups. A detailed explanation of the types of interviews was explained. The types of interviews section was followed by the procedures for writing effective interview questions and the process of conducting interviews. Writing the interview procedures sections was then explicated and that was followed by the directions for analyzing the interviews data. The last section detailed how to write up the findings for the research.

Chapter Highlights

Two popular approaches used to gather information are interviews and focus groups. Both approaches involve real-time conversations with the participants and are qualitative data techniques that can provide rich and deep information regarding the problem of practice Interviews and focus groups can elicit rich and deep information where other data collection methods may fall short.

An interview is a conversation between an interviewer and interviewee.

A focus group is a form of person-to-group communication, and it is also a way of collecting rich and detailed information; however, focus groups tend to be less personal.

Three type of interviews are structured, unstructured, or semi-structured.

A structured interview is a formal data collection method that employs a series of pre-set interview questions.

An unstructured interview is best described as an informal conversation or chat.

A semi-structured interview is a combination of structured and unstructured interviews.

Interview questions need to be grounded in the literature.

Use open-ended questions in interviews.

Pitfalls to avoid when writing interview questions include:

Avoid leading questions

Avoid loaded questions

Avoid push questions

Avoid double-barreled questions

Avoid absolute questions

Avoid poorly worded questions

Avoid long questions

Steps for conducting interviews:

Step 1. Ensure accessibility

Step 2. Get permission to conduct the research

Step 3. Identify your participants for the interview

Step 4. Select sampling procedures

Step 5. Secure logistics

Step 6. Record the interview

Step 7. Include opening statements

Step 8. Collect demographic information

Step 9. Ask the interview questions

Step 10. Include closing statements

Begin the procedures section of the educational report with an overview of the section. This section may cover multiple approaches (such as interviews, focus groups, etc.). The Overview should begin with a brief restatement of the nature and purpose of the study in relationship to the educational site.

Data should be analyzed immediately after it is gathered (such as after interviews are completed).

Transcribing is the process of putting human speech into written form.

Script dialog is similar to the dialog between characters in a movie script or screen play.

Coding is a systematic process of identifying key passages and text then making relationships between the words, phrases, and concepts.

Themes are prominent ideas that surface from the transcriptions. Themes should be specified and related directly to the research questions.

The Findings Section for applied research may contain multiple analyses. For that reason, begin the findings section of the educational report with an overview of the section. The Overview should begin with a brief restatement of the nature and purpose of the study in relationship to the educational site. Following the relationship to the site, the different analyses that will be used will be presented. The Findings Section should be organized by approach.

CHAPTER 6

Surveys

Objectives

By the end of this chapter, the reader will be able to:

- Define survey research
- Describe the various types of survey scales
- Identify examples of various types of survey scales
- Explain forced ranking
- Write appropriate survey questions
- Differentiate between poor and good survey questions
- Develop a demographic survey
- List the steps for conducting a survey
- Recognize different sampling procedures/methods

Key Terms

- Checklist
- Closed-ended
- Convenience sampling
- Forced ranking scale
- Frequency scale
- Likert scale
- Multiple-choice

Introduction

Surveys serve as a means of collecting data quickly and easily from large numbers of participants. **Survey research** is the systematic collection of data about participants' beliefs, behaviors, practices, opinions, or attitudes using a customized, standardized, and structured format. The surveys are standardized in that each participant receives the same survey that is presented in the same manner. Surveys used in applied research may generate information that is precise, expedient, and easy, as compared to other forms of data collection. However, although surveys are quick and easy to initiate, they typically do not elicit rich and deep information that an in-person interview may permit. One aspect of survey research that is critical to remember is that the goal of your survey is to solve the problem of practice. It is easy to lose track of your purpose, and when that happens, researchers typically collect data that is not relevant. In this chapter, you will learn about different types of survey scales, writing survey questions, the steps required to conduct a survey, and writing the data collection procedures and findings sections of your educational report.

Various Types of Survey Scales

There are many different types of scales used to collect data, and each type may yield very different information. It is extremely important to thoughtfully and skillfully choose the correct or most appropriate type of scale for your study. Below are some of the most common types of scales used in applied research. Remember to always remain focused on solving the problem of practice as you consider the type or types of scale for your quantitative survey.

Likert Scale

The **Likert scale** provides a prompt and the participant is expected to indicate the degree to which he or she agrees or disagrees with the given prompt. A Likert scale prompt could be used when the researcher desires to measure the attitudes or opinions on an assumed linear continuum from strongly agree to strongly disagree, with the neutral point being neither agree nor disagree (McLeod, 2015). Likert scales are popular because they reveal the degree of a belief, opinion, or attitude about a given topic. They are also popular because they are simple, and they are easy for the researcher to create and the participant to respond to. Below are examples of Likert scale questions.

Example 1 of a Likert scale survey question:

(Instructions: Mark one of the following.)

Hiring procedures utilized in the school district are time-costly.
☐ Strongly Agree   ☐ Agree   ☐ Neutral   ☐ Disagree   ☐ Strongly Disagree

Example 2 of a Likert scale survey question:

(Instructions: Mark one of the following.)

Increased administrator support would reduce student behavior referrals.
☐ Strongly Agree   ☐ Agree   ☐ Neutral   ☐ Disagree   ☐ Strongly Disagree

Other response options are permissible and may include Likert scale options such as:

☐ Very Good ☐ Good ☐ Neutral ☐ Poor ☐ Very Poor
☐ Always ☐ Often ☐ Sometimes ☐ Rarely ☐ Never

When composing Likert scale prompts, notice that these prompts are written in the form of a statement rather than a question. Writing prompts like this allow the degree of agreement or disagreement to be distinguished. Additionally, you should create questions that avoid a neutral response as much as possible so that you obtain data that makes the most difference for your research. Ideally, multiple Likert scale questions would be included in a survey to obtain optimal data results, and questions should be diversified to represent an adequate range of opinions to avoid causing or limit potential bias in the results.

Multiple Choice

Multiple-choice questions typically consist of one or two sentences followed by four or five response options from which the participant must choose, though more or fewer response options may be included. You may decide to use multiple choice questions when you want participants to choose answers from a list of response options you provide. Multiple-choice questions are popular because they are intuitive and can yield data that is quick and easy to analyze. For the multiple-choice prompt or question format, you may decide to allow participants to choose only one response option per question via a *single-response option* or multiple responses via a *multiple-response option*. Below are examples of both a single-response option and a multiple-response option.

Example of a Multiple-Choice Question using *"Single-Response:"*

(Instructions: Mark one of the following.)

Students who are _____ tend to score higher on the OEA for Science?
☐ musical-rhythmic
☐ visual-spatial
☐ verbal-linguistic
☐ logical-mathematical
☐ bodily-kinesthetic

Example of a Multiple-Choice Question using *"Multiple-Responses:"*

(Instructions: Mark all that apply.)

Students who receive _____ support tend to score higher on the OEA for Science?
☐ parental
☐ teacher
☐ counselor
☐ administrative

When constructing response options for multiple-choice questions, you may decide to force participants to choose from a fixed list of response options that you have predetermined, or you may choose to add another option called "other." Adding the "other" option relieves a common drawback of using multiple-choice questions in that having solely fixed option responses does not allow participants the opportunity to express themselves completely or provide any information beyond the response options given in the question, which can bias the research. In other words, questions might be written in a manner that is biased toward a certain outcome. Adding the "other" response option allows participants to specify the answer if their choice for a response option is not included in the list. Following is an example of adding the "other" option.

Examples of a Multiple-Choice Question using *"Other-Response"* **option:**
(Instructions: Mark all that apply.)

Students who receive _____ support tend to score higher on the OEA for Science?
☐ parental
☐ teacher
☐ counselor
☐ other (please specify) _____

A word of caution about including the "other" response option. If you choose to include too many "other" options for participants, it may weaken your ability to make comparisons between response options made by all participants. Be selective when including the "other" option.

True or False Questions

A **true or false question** presents information that requires the participant to decide whether the information presented is either a true statement or a false statement. When appropriate, the True or False may be replaced with Yes or No answers. True or false questions can be beneficial in applied research since these questions are a quick and easy means of obtaining information from participants. This type of question allows the participant to complete the survey question in a minimum amount of time as compared to other question types. However, constructing effective true or false questions that yield relevant information to help solve a problem in practice may be challenging, and if not carefully planned and worded, true or false questions may return information that does not help solve the problem in practice. Thus, if you choose to include true or false questions in your survey, you need to know the specific reason for doing so. Trying to establish a connection between your true or false question and the problem of practice will increase the chances that you will gather data that may lend to a solution to the problem. Worded effectively, any of these options may yield data relevant to the study, and poorly worded questions may yield irrelevant or ineffective data. Below are a few examples of true or false questions.

Example of a True or False survey question:
(Instructions: Mark one of the following.)

Students receive high quality instruction.
☐ True
☐ False

When creating true or false questions, make sure that you are only asking the participant to respond to only one thing within each prompt. For example, the following is an example of a true or false question to avoid since the participant may want to answer true to one part of the prompt and false to the other.

Example of an ineffective True or False question:

Students receive high quality instruction and new curriculum to help improve OEA scores.
☐ True
☐ False

This question should be avoided because the participant may want to state that the students receive high quality instruction, but that they do not receive new curriculum or vice versa. Avoid writing true or false questions that ask about multiple things or multiple levels.

Checklist

A **checklist** is a straightforward way of collecting participant data concerning how a topic is perceived by the participant and typically includes a list of adjectives. A checklist could be used when you want to know multiple adjectives that a participant would use to describe a specific topic rather than the degree to which the participant feels about the topic. One advantage of a checklist is that it is simple to write and respond to. Another advantage of a checklist is that one question may solicit multiple responses, which may allow you to draw conclusions using multiple data points rather than a single response question. The disadvantage is that it does not allow the participant to explicitly state the degree he or she feels about the topic to be disclosed. When writing a checklist prompt, remember that every adjective chosen should be included for a specific reason. Do not just simply write a list of random adjectives; rather, make sure you have weighed the logic behind each adjective choice to determine what data you may glean from a participant choosing each particular adjective on the list. This will lead to more robust information that may lend to solving the problem in practice. Below is an example of a checklist prompt.

Example of a Checklist question:

(Instructions: Put an x in the space before every word you believe describes your current teaching practices for kindergarten language arts skills.)

☐ Accurate	☐ Effective	☐ Irrelevant
☐ Applicable	☐ Frustrating	☐ Skillful
☐ Appropriate	☐ Inadequate	☐ Stimulating
☐ Bad	☐ Insufficient	☐ Systematic
☐ Challenging	☐ Logical	☐ Unproductive
☐ Constructive	☐ Positive	☐ Unsuccessful
☐ Costly	☐ Practical	☐ Well planned

Notice that there are multiple opposing adjectives included. This is intentional, as it offers the participant diverse options from which to choose. If most of the options are similar, it would skew the results.

Forced Ranking

A **forced ranking scale** is a prompt that forces the participant to rank each given item in the prompt using ordinals. Ranking prompts force the participant to establish an ordinal relationship between prompts; thus, this scale should be used when you want to limit the number of responses a participant may choose from and you want the items ranked *in order*. This type of query would be used when the order is imperative to the research results. When creating a forced ranking scale, it is important to present a logical number of prompts. Since participants are ranking items, this requires them to read completely through the list before making a first selection. Then, they must read it again to make a second selection and a third. If you include 20 prompts, you are not likely to get accurate results as participants may get frustrated with reading and rereading the prompts. Limit the number of options to only the number necessary to gain the data that is needed to solve the problem. It is recommended that no more than 10 prompts be included. Following is an example of a forced ranking scale.

Example of a Forced Ranking survey question:

> **Instruction:** Rank each item below in the order of importance that you believe will have the most impact on improving OEA scores. Rank the items from 1 to 5 with one being the item you believe will have the most significant impact and five being the one you believe will have the least amount of impact on OEA scores.
>
> _____ professional development
> _____ teaching supports
> _____ parental involvement
> _____ new curriculum
> _____ more designated instructional time

One disadvantage of forced ranking is that the intervals between prompts do not necessarily have the same value per participant. For example, two participants may have marked that parental involvement and new curriculum were their number one and number two choices respectively. However, one participant may truly value parental involvement, and though his or her second choice was new curriculum, he or she may believe that the only option that will change OEA scores is more parental involvement, but since he or she was forced to rank the items, this number two ranking may have a totally different value than the other participant who ranked new curriculum as the second most important prompt to improve OEA scores. The second participant may believe that parental involvement and new curriculum are almost equal in importance to improving OEA scores but still had to rank them, so that participant selected one over the other without really considering them to be different in terms of importance. Thus, the disadvantage of forced ranking scales is differing interval values. If you choose to use a forced ranking scale for your survey, make sure that you need to know the order of a participants' preference but do not need the interval measurement.

Frequency Scale

A **frequency scale** is a form of data collection that allows participants to indicate how often they have taken an action. There may be reasons that you, as the researcher, need to know the frequency that a particular behavior has occurred in order to help solve a problem in practice. If so, this is when you would use a frequency scale. For example, if you are trying to determine if professional development would help increase OEA scores, it may be helpful to know how often (the frequency) participants have participated in professional development training in the past. An advantage of frequency scales is that they are quick and easy to use. Data analysis of this type of tool also allows you to compare frequencies of actions among participants, and it allows you to provide for five different behavior frequencies. The prompt must specify the time period in which the behavior or activity occurs. An example of a frequency scale is below.

Example of a Frequency Scale survey question:

> **Instruction:** Write in the number of times you do each of the things listed below in the space to the right of each statement.
> How many times do you do the following things _each week_ in your classroom?
>
> Teach specifically to the OEA.. _____
> Incorporate additional curriculum to prepare for the OEA.................................. _____
> Administer practice-style quizzes to prepare students for the OEA...................... _____
> Assign students OEA homework assignments .... _____

Go to *www.khlearn.com* to watch a video about types of surveys.

How to Write the Survey Questions

When developing survey questions, you should skillfully compose the questions with the goal of answering the central question of your study. Developing quality survey questions can take time, and you should contemplate and refine each question until they are just right. Below are tips to help you develop quality survey questions.

Ground the questions in the literature: Surveys must be grounded in the literature. Before constructing survey questions, a thorough and complete review of the literature must be conducted. In general, it is recommended that researchers read at least a few hundred peer-reviewed journal articles to become vastly familiar with the evidence presented in the literature. Furthermore, most applied research studies should include and cite a few hundred peer-reviewed scholarly references. You must ground the research questions in the literature. In other words, survey questions are derived from what you discovered during the literature review. For applied research, the survey will be generated from the most current research and evidence found in a review of the current literature, which are sources that were published within the past five years. Surveys generated will allow for the most pertinent information to be solicited in order to help formulate a solution to the problem in practice you are researching. Grounded in the literature, or supported by the literature, means that you have conducted a thorough investigation of the current literature regarding the problem in practice, and then survey questions are formulated from evidence based on the literature review. Each survey question is supported with at least one citation to denote the source or sources from which the survey question is grounded or derived, though multiple citations are ideal and recommended. Below are two survey question examples that are considered grounded in the literature regarding "low OEA scores" as the problem in practice.

Do you believe professional development for teachers impacts students' OEA scores?
☐ Yes
☐ No

This question is appropriate because it is grounded in or supported by the literature. Below is a citation that establishes evidence for including a survey question regarding professional development for teachers in relation to low OEA scores.

"Question two referenced professional development, and according to McGuinn (2016), the Every Student Succeeds Act focus remained on high-need areas of learning and improved professional development for teachers."

Though brief, this sentence establishes that the literature revealed that improved professional development may increase OEA scores. Including this question may reveal if participants of this study believe OEA scores would improve if teachers participated in additional professional development.

Use closed-ended questions: Questions for surveys are usually **closed-ended** meaning that participants must choose from a predetermined list of responses. Closed-ended questions are often used in survey data collection even though, in certain situations, open-ended questions may be appropriate and are presented in the form of fill-in-the-blank or short answer questions. However, this chapter will focus on closed-ended survey questions. Below is an example of a closed-ended survey question.

Teacher instructional supports may help increase students' OEA scores.
☐ Strongly Agree   ☐ Agree   ☐ Neutral   ☐ Disagree   ☐ Strongly Disagree

Notice that the participant must choose from the five response options given, and there is not an option for the participant to elaborate in his or her own words.

Tips for Writing Survey Questions

Survey questions need to be created to elicit the information that is needed to help the researcher formulate a solution to the problem of practice. Below are some pitfalls to avoid when creating survey questions.

Avoid Leading Questions: A leading question subtly influences the survey participant to answer a certain way by assuming a particular experience, situation, or outcome that may or may not be true. For example, the question below is a poor question because the word "bad" in the responses implies that participant's high school experience was somehow unpleasant. This may or may not be true. The better question below the poor question removes the bias and makes the question neutral.

Poor Question:

How bad was your high school experience?
- ☐ Not Bad
- ☐ Bad
- ☐ Neutral
- ☐ Somewhat Bad
- ☐ Very bad

Better Question:

How would you describe your high school experience?
- ☐ Not Bad
- ☐ Bad
- ☐ Neutral
- ☐ Good
- ☐ Very Good

Avoid Loaded Questions: A loaded question is one that implies that the survey participant engaged in an activity or attended a situation that is controversial, unjust, or illegal. For example, the first question below is a poor question because it assumes the participant engages in an illegal activity. This type of question may discourage the participants from continuing in the survey. A better question would use a qualifying question. By doing so, you will provide the participant the opportunity to dispute the claim.

Poor Question:

How often do you use illegal drugs during school?
- ☐ Once a week
- ☐ Twice a week
- ☐ Three times a week
- ☐ More than three times a week

Better Question (with qualifier):

Do you use illegal drugs? ☐ Yes ☐ No
If yes, how often do you use illegal drugs during school?
- ☐ Once a week
- ☐ Twice a week
- ☐ Three times a week
- ☐ More than three times a week

Avoid Push Questions: A push question tricks the survey participant into answering the question in a certain way. Unlike a leading question, the researcher is aware of the implications of the question and purposely tries to get an answer to support their claim. For example, the first question below is a poor question because it forces the survey participant to agree with the researcher's presupposition that the "teacher is incompetent." This type of question is unethical. The better question removes any innuendos or opinions and makes the question neutral.

Poor Question:

Rumor has it that your teacher is incompetent; how do you feel about his ability to communicate?

☐ Very Good   ☐ Good   ☐ Neutral   ☐ Poor   ☐ Very Poor

Better Question:

How do you feel about your teacher's ability to communicate?

☐ Very Good   ☐ Good   ☐ Neutral   ☐ Poor   ☐ Very Poor

Avoid Double-Barreled Questions: The double-barreled question touches on two or more subjects within the same question. For example, the first question below is a poor question because it asks the survey participant to describe both "breakfast and lunch" at the same time. This type of question may confuse the answer because the survey participants may have different opinions regarding each dining experience. A better option would be to use two separate questions (as shown in the better question).

Poor Question:

How would you describe the cafeteria's food during breakfast and lunch?

☐ Very Good   ☐ Good   ☐ Neutral   ☐ Poor   ☐ Very Poor

Better Questions:

How would you describe the cafeteria's food during breakfast?

☐ Very Good   ☐ Good   ☐ Neutral   ☐ Poor   ☐ Very Poor

How would you describe the cafeteria's food during lunch?

☐ Very Good   ☐ Good   ☐ Neutral   ☐ Poor   ☐ Very Poor

Avoid Absolute Questions: An absolute question contains absolute terms such as all, never, always, everybody, no one, only, etc., and it focuses the participant's attention on unrealistic events or situations. For example, the first question below is a poor question because it asks the survey participant to assume an unrealistic group of "every" student. The participant may disagree with the absoluteness of the questions discrediting it as an extreme case and in turn may cause uncertainty in the reply. A better question would be to avoid absolutes.

Poor Question:

Do you believe *every* student cheats on his or her exams?

☐ Yes

☐ No

Better Question:

Do you believe students cheat on their exams?

☐ Yes

☐ No

Avoid Poorly Worded Questions: A poorly worded question uses words that are confusing, unclear, and/or inappropriate for a particular audience; the question uses the words that are not within the survey participant's vocabulary or are poor word choices. For example, the first question given is a poorly worded question because it uses the word "delineate." Some participants may be unaware of the meaning of the word. A better question would use a simpler word.

Poor Question:

How would you delineate your college experience?

☐ Very Poor

☐ Poor

☐ Neutral

☐ Good

☐ Very Good

Better Question:

How would you rate your college experience?

☐ Very Poor

☐ Poor

☐ Neutral

☐ Good

☐ Very Good

Avoid Long Questions: Long questions are not concise and may cause the participants to get tired or bored. The researcher should use well-written and succinct sentences. For example, the first question below is wordy. A better question would be shorter and succinct.

Poor Question:

Because of the tremendous increase in computer use among students and the rise of artificial intelligence, do you believe that artificial intelligence should be used in the class room?

☐ Yes

☐ No

Better Question:

Do you believe that artificial intelligence should be used in the class room?

☐ Yes

☐ No

 Go to *www.khlearn.com* to watch a video about writing survey questions.

Developing Demographic Questions

It is important to collect demographic information when conducting a survey in order to determine if groups of people behave or respond in similar ways. Demographic information common to research include age, sex, and ethnicity; these three items are often referred to as the "Big Three." For applied research, other demographic information may be needed, such as the participant's job title, type of education, years of experience, grade level, socioeconomic status, etc. When conducting a survey, only collect demographic information that is relevant to your study and no more. It is important to keep focused on solving the specific problem of practice when developing demographic questions. To help get ideas for effective demographic questions, consider visiting the U.S. government's Census Bureau website and websites from other professional organizations. For applied research, demographic questions need to be written clearly and concisely to solicit information needed for the study. Categories of demographic information that survey questions may include (but are not limited to) the following:

Age	Years of experience
Gender	Religion
Race or ethnicity	Socioeconomic status
Job title or position	Marital status
Annual income	Family size
Time employed	Location
Education	Grade level
Type of education	Living arrangement
Parents' education	Primary language spoken

Constructing demographic questions precisely is the key to receiving the information you need for your research. Below is an example of a poorly worded demographic question. This question is indirect and has unnecessary words. It appears to be convoluted and may confuse participants.

Race: Are you White, Black or African-American, American Indian or Alaskan Native, Asian, Native Hawaiian or other Pacific Islander, or some other race?

☐ White

☐ Black or African-American

☐ American Indian or Alaskan Native

☐ Asian

☐ Native Hawaiian or other Pacific islander

☐ From multiple races

☐ Some other race (please specify)

Notice the difference between the above poorly written demographic question and the concisely written question below. The question below gets straight to the point. It requires less effort to understand what the question is asking, which makes it quick to read and easy for the participant to provide a response.

What is your race?

☐ White

☐ Black or African-American

☐ American Indian or Alaskan Native

☐ Asian

☐ Native Hawaiian or other Pacific islander

☐ From multiple races

☐ Some other race (please specify) _____

When constructing your demographic questions, write concisely, be specific, and ask the exact questions you want the participant to answer. Make the survey questions straightforward for the participant. Following is an example of correctly written demographic questions. As you examine the example questions, notice that the demographic questions are grouped by type. The first three questions inquire about age, race, and gender, which ask about the physicality of the participant. Questions four, five, and six inquire about the educational experiences of the participant. Grouping demographic questions by type is an effective way to present the survey questions as it does not require the participants' thoughts to unnecessarily deviate back and forth between subjects.

See Demographic Questions example below:

Demographic Questions

Instructions: Mark one answer for each demographic question.

1. Which category best describes your age in years?
   - ( ) 21–29
   - ( ) 30–39
   - ( ) 40–49
   - ( ) 50–59
   - ( ) 60 or older

2. What is your race?
   - ( ) White
   - ( ) Black/African-American
   - ( ) Asian
   - ( ) Native Hawaiian/other Pacific Islander
   - ( ) From multiple races
   - ( ) Other race (please specify): _____

3. What is your sex?
   - ( ) Female
   - ( ) Male

4. What is the highest educational level you have achieved?
   - ( ) Less than high school diploma or equivalent (e.g., did not graduate and no GED)
   - ( ) High school diploma or equivalent (e.g., GED)
   - ( ) Associate degree
   - ( ) Bachelor's degree
   - ( ) Graduate degree
   - ( ) Doctorate

5. How many years of teaching experience do you have?
   - ( ) 1–3 years
   - ( ) 4–8 years
   - ( ) 9–15 years
   - ( ) 16–25 years
   - ( ) More than 26 years

6. What grade(s) do you teach? (You may select more than one response).
   - ( ) 1st grade
   - ( ) 2nd grade
   - ( ) 3rd grade
   - ( ) 4th grade
   - ( ) 5th grade
   - ( ) 6th grade
   - ( ) 7th grade
   - ( ) 8th grade
   - ( ) 9th grade
   - ( ) 10th grade
   - ( ) 11th grade
   - ( ) 12th grade
   - ( ) I am not a classroom teacher
   - ( ) Other, specify _____

Creating a Questionnaire

After you have chosen your survey questions, you will put the survey together. The survey should be intuitive and easy to read. Most effective surveys have from 10 to 20 questions and take less than 10 minutes to complete. By keeping your survey short, you will help participants avoid survey fatigue.

The questionnaire should contain a title followed by instructions. The instructions should briefly explain why the survey is being conducted and how the information will be used. Include information on how to complete the survey. Within the questionnaire, instructions for answering each question should be provided. Include instructions for each question type, keeping in mind that question types should be purposefully chosen. If the survey has multiple pages, instruction located at the top of each page should state so, also include the number of questions, and the time it will take to finish the survey. Include in the instruction *how* and *when* to return the survey and end by thanking the participants for agreeing to participate in the survey. Below is an example of an appropriate questionnaire that includes the demographic questions and content-specific questions. This survey utilizes a Likert scale question format. Note that many of the survey question types from before could have been chosen. This example is simply to provide a visual example of what a quantitative survey for an applied research could look like.

Improving Students' OEA Scores Survey

Instructions: Your school's leadership team is looking into ways to improve students' OEA scores. By participating in the survey, you can help with this effort. The survey is confidential, and the information will be used to help inform the leadership regarding improving OEA scores. Complete the survey using either pencil or pen. This survey has 15 questions and takes approximately 5 minutes to complete. Survey responses should be completed within 5 days and returned to the school secretary. Thank you again for participating.

Demographic Questions
(Mark only one answer for each question.)

1. Which category best describes your age in years?
   - ( ) 21–29
   - ( ) 30–39
   - ( ) 40–49
   - ( ) 50–59
   - ( ) 60 or older
2. What is your race?
   - ( ) White
   - ( ) Black/African-American
   - ( ) Asian
   - ( ) Native Hawaiian/other Pacific Islander
   - ( ) From multiple race
   - ( ) Other race (please specify): _____
3. What is your gender?
   - ( ) Female
   - ( ) Male

4. What is the highest educational level you have obtained?
   - ( ) Less than high school diploma or equivalent
   - ( ) High school diploma or equivalent (e.g., GED)
   - ( ) Associate degree
   - ( ) Bachelor's degree
   - ( ) Master's degree
   - ( ) Doctorate
5. What grade(s) do you teach? (You may select more than one).
   - ( ) Kindergarten
   - ( ) 1st grade
   - ( ) 2nd grade
   - ( ) 3rd grade
   - ( ) 4th grade
   - ( ) 5th grade
   - ( ) 6th grade
   - ( ) 7th grade
   - ( ) 8th grade
   - ( ) 9th grade
   - ( ) 10th grade
   - ( ) 11th grade
   - ( ) 12th grade
   - ( ) I am not a classroom teacher
   - ( ) Other (specify) _____

Content Questions
(Mark only one answer for each question.)

1. Students with low OEA scores are most likely to be members of what socioeconomic group?
   - ( ) A high-income socioeconomic group
   - ( ) A medium-income socioeconomic group
   - ( ) A low-income socioeconomic group
   - ( ) Socioeconomic group does not affect OEA scores
2. Teacher retention impacts students' OEA scores.
   - ( ) Strongly Agree
   - ( ) Agree
   - ( ) Neither Agree or Disagree
   - ( ) Disagree
   - ( ) Strongly Disagree
3. Schools with low OEA scores have _____.
   - ( ) high teacher absenteeism
   - ( ) average teacher absenteeism
   - ( ) low teacher absenteeism
   - ( ) teacher absenteeism does not affect OEA scores.
4. Students with low OEA scores have received _____.
   - ( ) high quality instruction
   - ( ) average quality instruction
   - ( ) low quality instruction
   - ( ) instruction quality has no impact on OEA scores

5. Teacher pay impacts students' OEA scores.
   - ( ) Strongly Agree
   - ( ) Agree
   - ( ) Neither Agree or Disagree
   - ( ) Disagree
   - ( ) Strongly Disagree
6. Instructional support for teachers impacts students' OEA scores.
   - ( ) Strongly Agree
   - ( ) Agree
   - ( ) Neutral
   - ( ) Disagree
   - ( ) Strongly Disagree
7. Teachers who successfully prepare their students for the OEA receive a(n) _____.
   - ( ) high amount of professional development
   - ( ) average amount of professional development
   - ( ) low amount of professional development
   - ( ) professional development does not affect OEA scores.
8. "New" English language arts curriculum will impact students' OEA scores.
   - ( ) Strongly Agree
   - ( ) Agree
   - ( ) Neither Agree or Disagree
   - ( ) Disagree
   - ( ) Strongly Disagree
9. Students' English language arts instructional time impacts students' OEA scores.
   - ( ) Strongly Agree
   - ( ) Agree
   - ( ) Neither Agree or Disagree
   - ( ) Disagree
   - ( ) Strongly Disagree
10. Students who receive parental support tend to score _____ on the OEA?
    - ( ) higher
    - ( ) average
    - ( ) lower
    - ( ) Parental support does not affect OEA scores

Conducting a Survey

After you have created your questionnaire, you are ready to send it out and collect data. Surveys can be conducted either electronically or physically. However, survey data collection should follow established protocol.

Step 1. Ensure accessibility: Accessibility is the ability of participants to be easily reached. Lack of access to personnel who may have key information to solving the problem of practice may result in inadequate solutions. Since many educational studies are conducted in an educational setting, you will be wise to consider school breaks, such as summer and traditional holidays, as most educators and students will not be available for research during those times. Summer break oftentimes represents a two- to three-month break in many school systems, and those months are potentially a period when participants are not likely available; this can significantly delay the research. Holidays are another time frame to consider. Though you may be off work during the holidays and have plenty of time to conduct interviews, most teachers, and students will not agree to be interviewed since, from their perspective, this is work-related and they are on a break.

Step 2. Get permission to conduct the research: Permission is the act of securing approval or authorization to conduct the research from leadership at the organization being studied. This is often referred to as site approval and should be obtained in writing. While seeking permission, the site leadership should be informed about the nature of the study, personnel who will be involved in the study, the length of the study, and what will be done with the information. Again, approval to conduct a survey must come from a person with appropriate site authority and should be obtained in writing. Some organizations may require Institutional Review Board (IRB) approval before research is conducted; however, if the applied research is site-specific, the results and solution to the problem are not generalizable beyond the site, and the project will not be published or disseminated beyond the site; most organizations will not require IRB.

Step 3. Identify the Participants: **Participants** are humans from whom a researcher obtains information. In applied research, identifying participants who are best qualified to provide information regarding the problem of practice is extremely important. Researchers often select a sample that "suits the purposes of the study and that is convenient" (Gall et al., 2006, p. 175). For applied research, surveys must include as many respondents as possible. As the researcher, you will need to determine the sample of participants who are most likely to offer information that will help solve the problem in practice. **Sampling** simply means "taking part of some population to represent the whole population" (Alrek & Settle, 1995, p. 54). For applied research, you may choose to survey the entire population or a small sample of the population associated with the problem. For example, if you are trying to solve the problem of low teacher attendance for a small rural school, the sample population may include one administrator, one counselor, and 11 teachers. This may comprise the entire faculty and staff of a small school. However, if you are trying to solve the same problem but for an entire large inner-city school district, you will only be able to choose a sample of the population to survey. You need to send out enough surveys to receive enough data that is representative of the entire population and with enough accuracy to make confident decisions regarding the results.

Step 4. Identify the Sampling Procedures: Choosing participants is a very important element of your research, as this is where data originates to help formulate a solution to the problem in practice that you are researching. Below are some types of participant sampling procedures used to determine participants for a survey. Participant selection methods should follow the recommendations of established researchers in the field and must be appropriately cited in the methods section of your study. According to Alreck and Settle (1995), "a random sample is the most desirable kind [of sampling procedure] for almost every survey... The random sample is best because it's most representative of the entire population. It's least likely to result in bias" (p. 70). Though random sampling is a great choice for many applied studies, it will not work in some studies. For example, if you are trying to solve a problem in a small school with a limited number of teachers, there may not be enough potential participants to allow for a random selection of participants. When deciding on which type of sampling procedure to choose for your study, stay focused on solving the problem and soliciting the participants that have the most relevant data to help you solve the problem. This may require purposeful or convenience sampling. Whichever sampling procedure you choose, be intentional and methodical. Below is a list of potential sampling procedures you may want to consider for your survey.

Purposeful sampling: **Purposeful sampling** means that the researcher selects individuals as participants because they can purposefully inform an understanding of the research problem (Creswell, 2013). Purposeful sampling helps to ensure the selected participants are information-rich (Patton, 2002), which may lend to solving the problem in practice. It is arguably the most utilized form of sampling in applied research.

Convenience sampling: **Convenience sampling** "saves time, money, and effort, but at the expense of information and credibility" (Creswell & Poth, 2018, p. 159). This is the least desirable form of sampling for applied research, but may be the only way of soliciting participants. When choosing participants using convenience sampling, it is advisable to include a statement in the results section of the final educational report advising readers to exercise caution when drawing conclusions since a convenience sample may include participants who are not well-informed regarding the problem.

Random sampling: **Random sampling** is a means of selecting participants when each possible participant has an equal chance of being selected as a participant for the study (Alreck & Settle, 1995). For example, if the study is being conducted to try and solve the problem of insufficient special education services offered in a large urban school district with 24 total schools, every teacher associated with the problem would have the same chance of participating in the study, and no teacher would receive a preferential participation opportunity. This type of sampling disables the researcher's ability to only select participants who may be biased toward a particular outcome for a problem.

Step 5. Choose a data collection method: As the researcher, you will need to determine the method you will use to collect your survey data. Below are four possible options, and those options are listed in the order based on the method that is used most often first.

Electronic survey: Survey data can be collected in a variety of ways. One of the easiest and quickest ways to conduct a survey is electronically. This method allows you to post a survey to a website, such as Survey Monkey, and send participants a link to the survey. Participants simply click on the link and take the survey. Results are tabulated in Survey Monkey, which makes data analysis instantaneous. You may also use other electronic survey methods and websites to create a survey for data collection purposes.

Email: Another easy way to conduct a survey is by email; this method gets the information directly to the participants from you and allows the participants to directly respond to you, which is a pretty straight-forward process. This method may take more time than an electronic survey and it does not offer any form of data analysis or manipulation. You will need to manually analyze surveys that are completed and returned via email.

Telephone: A telephone call may serve as a means of surveying participants but is less direct than a web-hosted survey or an email survey. It also does not offer any form of automated data analysis. Phone calls may be recorded, but you must first have the permission of the respondent (along with IRB approval in some cases) to record calls.

Postal service: You may use the postal service to send paper surveys, but this method is not time efficient. This may be a necessary means of data collection necessary in areas where the internet is not a viable means of collecting data, such as remote geographical locations.

Remember, the fastest means of collecting survey data results may not always be the most effective way of collecting data. Remain focused on solving the problem in practice when making the decision as to which way you will collect survey data. It is better to have participants who are well-informed about the problem you are researching and collect information-rich data than it is to quickly collect irrelevant data.

Step 6. Send out the questionnaire: When contacting participants for your survey, you will need to address them in two ways. First is the invitation followed by the questionnaire. For example, email the participants an invitation regarding the survey with a link to the survey. See email below.

The purpose of this email is to request your participation in a survey regarding factors to improve student achievement on the Ohio Educational Assessment. The survey will take approximately 15 minutes to complete. To participate, please click on this Google form link: _____ and follow the instructions provided for this 15-question survey. Survey responses should be completed within 10 days of this email. Thank you for participating in this important survey.

Step 7. Collect the questionnaire: The key to a successful survey is having a high return rate. The participants need to be specifically instructed on *how* and *when* to take and return the survey. For example, if you are conducting an electronic survey, instruct the participants to click the "submit" button to conclude the survey. If clicking the submit button is required, make sure to clearly include that in the survey instructions and at the end of the survey. If the return rate is low, you may also consider sending out reminder notices to your participants. Include in the reminder notice *how* and *when* to return the survey. Finally, incentives, such as prizes and gift cards may help increase participation. Once a reasonable number of surveys have been returned, you may begin the data analysis process and present the findings.

 Go to *www.khlearn.com* to watch a video about conducting a survey.

Writing the Procedures: Survey

The procedures section for applied research may contain multiple approaches. For that reason, begin the procedure section of the educational report with an overview of the section. The Overview should begin with a brief restatement of the nature and purpose of the study in relation to the educational site. Then, introduce the different approaches that you will use. The Procedure Section should be organized by approach. The approach we will focus on in this section is surveys. An example of an Overview to the procedures section is below.

See Procedures Overview example below:

PROCEDURES

Overview

The purpose of this study was to provide recommendations to the leadership team at Hampton High School with possible solutions to the problem of students' low test scores on the Ohio Educational Assessment (OEA) for Science. Hampton High School is a mid-size suburban public high school in southeastern Ohio. This portion of the report provides interview procedures, survey procedures, and documents procedures.

Writing the Survey Procedures

Writing procedures for applied research is a step-by-step process; the procedures are presented in narrative form. When using a survey as an approach, you should include the various elements of the survey in your write-up. Begin by describing the type of survey questions you will use (e.g., Likert, multiple choice, true/false, etc.) and the method of data collection.

See Survey Procedures example below:

Survey Procedures

The second approach used to collect data in this study was a survey. This approach explored how science educators participating in a survey would solve the problem of low test scores on the Ohio Educational Assessment (OEA) for Science at a suburban public high school in southeastern Ohio. To collect data, a closed ended Likert scale survey was administered electronically using Survey Monkey, an internet-based program. A quantitative survey is an appropriate approach for data collection for this study since it provides participants with the opportunity to have one and only one answer to each question, while ensuring that there is, in fact, an answer to every question (Bickman & Rog, 2009).

Next include the sampling procedures and justification for why the sample was chosen. Data collection strategies must be defined in layman's terms and appropriateness to the study must be justified. You should suggest a time frame for administering and completing the survey. Also include how you will analyze the data in this section.

See sampling procedures below.

Participants included 13 teachers, one special education teacher, and two administrators at Hampton High. This was a purposeful sample because of the participants' familiarity with the science program (Creswell & Poth, 2019). The participants received an email with instructions regarding how to complete the survey. The email included the link to Survey Monkey, consent to participate, and instructions on how to complete the survey. The participants were given a two-week time frame in which to complete the survey; if more time was needed, arrangements were made. The results were analyzed by calculating the frequency of each number reported on the Likert scale on a question-by-question basis, as well as the average score reported by all participants for each question. The survey included demographic questions and 15 statements developed from the literature review, to which survey participants responded using a 5-point Likert scale rating. The prompts on the survey included the following questions.

Conclude with the survey questions. The survey questions or prompts must be stated, then justified and supported by the literature. Some questions may be "incidental" or not supported by the literature; however, a reason must still be given for including those questions. Demographic questions may also be addressed at this point or placed in the appendix of the educational report.

See Survey Questions example below:

Survey Questions

1. Classroom instruction is delivered with the same rigor specified in the NGSS standards.

5	4	3	2	1
Always	Often	Sometimes	Rarely	Never

This question sought to identify how well-aligned instruction is with the standards and the rigor of each. Ensuring that students are learning material, albeit scaffolded at the onset, at the same level at which they are expected to demonstrate mastery, leads to better standardized test performance (Drake & Burns, 2004).

2. Time is provided during contract hours for collaboration between teachers of the same courses.

5	4	3	2	1
Always	Often	Sometimes	Rarely	Never

Meeting with other teachers of the same course helps teachers to disaggregate data and provide insight into students' performance. This question was intended to identify the frequency of these meetings that occur during contract hours, when teachers are most likely to analyze data effectively and complete the task. Further, during this time, instructional decisions can be made, and the collaborative planning that occurs during these meetings can lead to improved lessons for all teachers (DuFour, 2004).

Checklist for the Survey Procedures

☐ Does the Survey Procedures include the type of survey (Likert scale, multiple choice, true/false, etc.) and its justification?

☐ Does the Survey Procedures include sampling type (purposeful sampling, snowball, etc.)?

☐ Does the Survey Procedures identify the participants?

☐ Does the Survey Procedures identify the rationale for participant selection?

☐ Does the Survey Procedures include how the survey was conducted?

☐ Does the Survey Procedures briefly explain data analysis procedures?

☐ Does the Survey Procedures include number of survey questions?

☐ Does the Survey Procedures include the survey questions and their rationale (the majority of questions should be cited using the literature)?

☐ The Survey Procedures is written in paragraph format.

☐ The Survey Procedures is written in past tense.

Writing the Survey Findings

The Findings Section for applied research may contain multiple analyses. For that reason begin the findings section of the educational report with an overview of the section. The Overview should begin with a brief restatement of the nature and purpose of the study in relationship to the educational site. Then, introduce the reader to the different analyses that will be used. The Findings Section should be organized by approach.

See Findings Overview example below:

FINDINGS

Overview

The purpose of this study was to provide recommendations to the leadership team at Hampton High School with possible solutions to the problem of low test scores on the Ohio Educational Assessment (OEA) for Science. This section of the report includes interview findings, survey findings, and documents findings.

The Survey Findings Write-Up

Begin writing the survey findings by describing the data collection procedure. Include the types of questions/scale used (e.g., Likert, multiple choice, true/false, etc.) and their scoring.

See Survey Findings example below:

Survey Findings

The second data collection approach was a survey. The survey contained demographic questions, as well as 15 Likert scale questions. The survey was administered via Survey Monkey. The scale consisted of five possible answers from Strongly Agree to Strongly Disagree and Always to Never.

Next, describe the participants. Provide the number of participants and pertinent demographic information. As a minimum, most demographic information should include the ages, sexes, and ethnicities of the participants.

See Survey Description of Participants example below:

Survey Description of Participants

Survey participants included 13 teachers at Hampton High School, as well as one special education teacher who worked directly with science, and two administrators, including principals. Of the 16 participants, 3 participants are in the 21 to 29 age range, 4 are in the 30 to 39 range, 4 are in the 40 to 49 range, 2 are in the 50 to 59 range, and 3 are in the 60 or older range. Five administrators participated, along with 2 special education educators, and 9 science teachers. Administrators' average years of service was 10.6 in their current role, while teachers, both special educators and science teachers, had an average tenure of 10.5 years, though it should be noted that two of the participants included in this statistic are in their first year at Hampton High School. Seven of the participants were male, while nine were female. The results of the surveys are reported in Tables 3.

After describing the participants, present the results in the form of figures and tables. Consider presenting the results in terms of frequency counts, percentages, and/or averages.

See Survey Results example below:

Survey Results

Table 3. Frequency and Average of Survey Responses

Question	Frequency					Avg.
	5	4	3	2	1	
1. Classroom instruction is delivered with the same rigor specified in the NGSS standards.	2	4	6	3	1	3.2
2. Time is provided during contract hours for collaboration between teachers of the *same* courses.	2	2	3	5	4	2.6
3. Data collected from both assessments are used to plan future instruction.	3	4	6	2	1	3.4
4. Content taught in each course is clearly communicated throughout the department.	6	6	2	1	1	3.9
5. Professional development focuses on new instructional strategies has been offered to science teachers.	0	1	3	5	7	1.9

Note: *Averages for each question was calculated by multiplying each response value by the corresponding Likert scale value and summing the results and then dividing the results by the total number of participant responses to the question.*

Example for question #5:

Likert scale	5	4	3	2	1
Response value	0	1	3	5	7
Sub total	0	4	9	10	7
Sum	30				
Participants	16				
Average	1.9				

Finally, end with a discussion of the findings and any takeaways that emerged from the survey. Use statistics, when appropriate, to support takeaways in the discussion section.

See Survey Discussion of the Findings example below:

Survey Discussion of the Findings

Two takeaways emerged. The themes include collaboration and professional development. Based on the survey data, questions 2, 5, 7, and 10 received the lowest ratings. All other questions received above average marks. Question 2 and 7 were of interest, which addressed collaboration. Questions 5 and 10 were of similar interest, which addressed professional development. In the survey, participants indicated that professional development specifically related to instructional strategies has not been offered to science teachers. In fact, question 5 scored an average of 1.9 out of 5—one of the lowest scores of any question on the survey. Because there is a lack of professional development to support instructional practices, it's reasonable to consider that a focus on more frequent professional development on the topic would strengthen instruction within the classroom, which would likely translate to improved scores on the OEA for Science at Hampton High School. Furthermore, meaningful data analysis conversations were another concern among the science faculty at Hampton High School. Participants reported that there is limited time allotted for data analysis conversation among teachers, evidenced by also receiving an average of 1.9 out of 5—another low score on the survey.

Checklist for the Survey Findings

☐ Does the Survey Findings include the type of scale?
☐ Does the Survey Findings include a brief overview of the procedures?
☐ Does the Survey Findings include a Description of Participants?
☐ Does the Survey Findings include Survey Results in the form of tables?
☐ Does the Survey Findings include a discussion of the findings and interpretation?
☐ Does the Survey Findings include a discussion of themes with supporting evidence?
☐ The Survey Findings is written in paragraph format.
☐ The Survey Findings is written in past tense.

Conclusion

Chapter 6 began with an introduction to survey research including the various types of scales. The scales were followed by the procedures for writing the survey questions and developing demographic questions. Creating a questionnaire was then explained along with how to conduct a survey. Writing the survey procedures was then detailed along with writing up the survey findings.

Chapter Highlights

Survey research is the systematic collection of data about participants' beliefs, behaviors, practices, opinions, or attitudes using a customized, standardized, and structured format.

Likert scales provide prompts and the participant is expected to indicate the degree to which he or she agrees or disagrees with the given prompts.

Multiple-choice questions typically consist of one or two sentences followed by four or five response options from which the participant must choose, though more or fewer response options may be included.

A true or false question presents information that requires participants to decide whether the information presented is either a true or false statement.

A checklist is a straightforward way of collecting participant data concerning how a topic is perceived by participants and typically includes a list of adjectives.

A forced ranking scale is a prompt that forces the participant to rank each given item in the prompt using ordinal numbers.

Frequency scale indicates how often an action has been done or taken by the participant.

Tips to help develop quality survey questions include: (1) ground the questions in the literature and (2) use closed-ended questions.

Pitfalls to avoid when creating survey questions include: (1) avoid leading questions, (2) avoid loaded questions, (3) avoid push questions, (4) avoid double-barreled questions, (5) avoid absolute questions, (6) avoid poorly worded questions, and (7) avoid long questions.

Demographic information common to most research is age, sex, and ethnicity; these three items are often referred to as "The Big Three."

Constructing demographic questions precisely is the key to receiving the information needed for your research.

Most effective surveys have 10 to 20 questions and take less than 10 minutes to complete.

The protocol for survey data collection involves the following steps: (1) ensure accessibility, (2) get permission to conduct the research, (3) identify the participants, (4) identify the sampling procedures, (5) choose a data collection method, (6) distribute the questionnaire, and (7) collect the questionnaire.

Some sampling procedures include purposeful sampling, convenience sampling, and random sampling.

Survey data may be distributed and collected electronically (over the internet or via email), by telephone, or via regular mail.

The Procedures and Findings sections of an educational report begin with an overview that has a brief restatement of the nature and purpose of the study in relationship to the educational site. Both sections should be organized.

Documents and Artifacts

Objectives

By the end of this chapter, the reader will be able to:

- Describe the differences between documents and artifacts
- Distinguish between primary sources and secondary sources
- Explain the steps involved in conducting a content analysis
- Differentiate between bar charts, trend charts, and frequency charts

Key Terms

- Artifacts
- Attributes
- Bar chart
- Content analysis
- Frequency Chart
- Primary source
- Secondary source
- Trend chart

Introduction

In applied research, data are all around us in the form of documents or artifacts. Both documents and artifacts contain factual and detailed information that can help us solve problems of practice. You, the researcher, must use reasonable judgment and consider the goals of your study before selecting documents or artifacts. When considering using documents and artifacts, you must assess the pros and cons of each type of data and how data will help to inform the problem of practice. The procedures and analysis used for documents and artifacts are very similar. In this chapter, you will learn the differences between documents and artifacts, the steps required to conduct a content analysis, and how to write the data collection procedures and findings sections of your educational report.

Differences between Documents and Artifacts

Documents and artifacts can come from both primary and secondary sources. A **primary source** is the original document or artifact under investigation, and it provides first-hand evidence. For example, a teacher's "original" grade book would be a primary source or document. On the other hand, a **secondary source** is an interpretation of an original document or artifact. For instance, if the school secretary collected all the grade books from each teacher in the school and then entered the grades into a spreadsheet, the grades in the spreadsheet would be considered a secondary source.

Documents are printed materials in either electronic or hard copy or written format that provide information and/or serve as official records. For example, documents can take the form of school policy manuals, attendance records, referral forms, electronic spread sheets, etc. On the other hand, **artifacts** are human-made physical objects that have personal, social, or cultural significance. For example, artifacts can take the form of photographs, artwork, school supplies, films, vinyl records, maps, computer software, etc. In applied research, selecting the documents and artifacts that best inform the problem of practice is extremely important. Both documents and artifacts can be either primary or secondary sources.

Conducting a Content Analysis

After identifying documents or artifacts to inform the research study, you will need to collect the materials and then search through the content to find patterns and trends in the data. You should consider using a **content analysis;** that is, a method for studying documents or artifacts by counting specific characteristics or attributes embedded in the source material and listing their frequency of occurrence. To conduct a content analysis, consider the following steps:

Step 1. Collect and organize the data: Before collecting documents or artifacts, you should consider the accessibility of the information. Lack of access may result in an inadequate solution to the problem of practice. For example, if student records are required to solve the problem, but the school cannot release the information due to the Family Educational Rights and Privacy Act (FERPA), then the information would be considered inaccessible. For this reason, you should consider accessibility before beginning the research. After you receive access to the documents or artifacts, collect the documents or artifacts, and label them by their content, date, and location from where you retrieved them.

Step 2. Look for common attributes: Examine the documents or artifacts and look for common attributes. **Attributes** are key features or characteristics of an object. Describe the attributes and make notes of their occurrence. For example, say you were considering a new dress codes policy for your school, and you began by examining the artifacts of student photos from past yearbooks. You may have observed and made note of the style, color, and length of the clothing. For documents, the same process applies, except that you are looking for common themes, concepts, and words. For example, you can look at the number of times the words male and female appear in the dress code policy manual for each year.

Step 3. Conduct a frequency count: Read through your notes and convert your observations into a frequency chart. A **frequency chart** is a table that shows the number of times an event or attribute appears within a data set. The frequency chart will allow you to graph the information and then find patterns in the data. For example, when examining student photos from past yearbooks, you may consider the presence of collars or no collars, sleeves or no sleeves, and the type of fabric pattern. See Table 1 for an example.

Table 1: *Frequency Chart: Clothing by Attribute and Year*

Year	2017	2018	2019	2020	2021
Collar	Yes (125) No (87)	Yes (130) No (89)	Yes (114) No (98)	Yes (130) No (100)	Yes (124) No (95)
Sleeve	Yes (130) No (99)	Yes (101) No (87)	Yes (134) No (149)	Yes (140) No (129)	Yes (100) No (121)
Pattern	Solid (100) Plaid (75) Floral (15) Striped (30)	Solid (123) Plaid (98) Floral (5) Striped (20)	Solid (120) Plaid (78) Floral (14) Striped (29)	Solid (130) Plaid (56) Floral (15) Striped (35)	Solid (130) Plaid (76) Floral (10) Striped (45)

Step 4. Make graphs and charts: Now, look for trends and patterns by visually representing the data using a bar chart or trend chart. A **bar chart** is a visual comparison of categorized data plotted by frequency, mean, median, etc. For example, Figure 1 below shows a bar chart that plots the collared shirts data from for each year's dress code from Step 3.

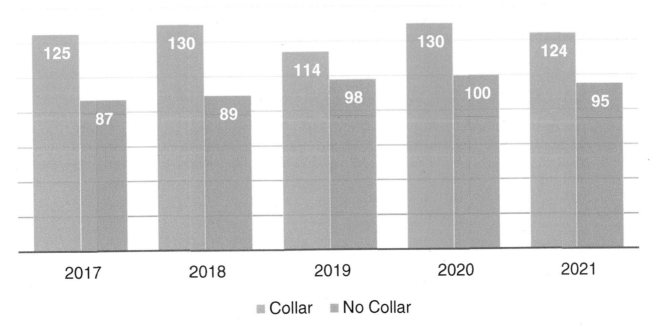

Dress Code: Collared Shirts

■ Collar ■ No Collar

Figure 1. Bar Chart showing collared skirt requirement for each year's dress code.
Source: Kurt Michael

Also, consider visually representing the data using a trend chart. A **trend chart** is a way to display data over time, for instance, plotting the fabric patterns over the five-year time period can be seen in Figure 2.

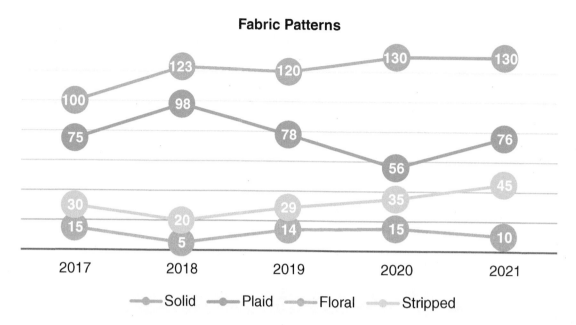

Figure 2. Trend chart showing fabric patterns over a five-year time period.
Source: Kurt Michael

Step 5. Look for trend and patterns in the data: Once the data have been plotted and critically reviewed, you should begin to identify patterns in the data. These patterns will emerge as trends, patterns, and themes. Trends, patterns, and themes should be specified and related to the research question.

Writing the Documents and Artifacts Procedures

The procedures section for applied research may contain multiple approaches. For that reason, begin the procedures section of the educational report with an overview of the section. The Overview should begin with a brief restatement of the nature and purpose of the study in relationship to the educational site. Then, introduce the reader to the different approaches that will be used. The Procedures Section should be organized by approach. The approach reviewed here is documents.

See Procedures Overview example below:

PROCEDURES

Overview

The purpose of this study was to provide recommendations to the leadership team at Hampton High School with possible solutions to the problem of students' low test scores on the Ohio Educational Assessment (OEA) for Science. Hampton High School is a mid-size suburban public high school in southeastern Ohio. This portion of the report provides interview procedures, survey procedures, and documents procedures.

Writing the Documents Procedures

Writing procedures for applied research is a step-by-step process, and the procedures are presented in narrative form. When using documents as an approach, you should include the various elements of the documents in your write-up. Begin by describing the type of documents you will collect. Include from where you will retrieve documents and the anticipated retrieval dates. Include why the documents are important in helping to inform the research regarding the problem of practice. End by explaining how you will analyze the data.

See the Documents Procedures example below:

Documents Procedures

The third approach used to collect data for this study was document analysis. This approach explored how a review of documents could inform the problem of low test scores on the Ohio Educational Assessment (OEA) for Science. A document is printed material in either electronic or hard copied written format that provides information and/or serves as an official record (Bickman & Rog, 2009). Archival data was retrieved from the ODOE website (ODOE, 2019). The site was used because it provided school data including test scores from the 2015–2016 school years through 2019–2020. This review of documents produced quantitative results and is important because it provides evidence of students' historical performance on the OEA for Science. The information is available to the public. Data gathered from this approach is presented in tabular format and as a trend chart.

Checklist for the Documents Procedures

- ☐ Does the Documents Procedures section include the type of document?
- ☐ Does the Documents Procedures section identify the rationale for using the documents?
- ☐ Does the Documents Procedures section include how the documents were obtained?
- ☐ Does the Documents Procedures section briefly explain how data were analyzed?
- ☐ The Documents Procedures section is written in paragraph format.
- ☐ The Documents Procedures section is written in past tense.

 Go to *www.khlearn.com* to watch a video about documents and artifacts.

Writing the Documents Findings

The Findings Section for applied research may contain multiple analyses. For that reason, begin the findings section of the educational report with an overview of the section. The Overview should begin with a brief restatement of the nature and purpose of the study in relationship to the educational site. Then introduce the reader to the different analyses that will be used. The Findings Section should be organized by approach.

See Findings Overview example below:

FINDINGS

Overview

The purpose of this study was to provide recommendations to the leadership team at Hampton High School with possible solutions to the problem of low test scores on the Ohio Educational Assessment (OEA) for Science. This section of the report includes interview findings, survey findings, and documents findings.

The Documents Findings Write-up

When using documents as an approach, you should include the various elements of the documents in your write-up. Begin by describing the type of documents used, where they came from, how they were retrieved, and the date or dates they were retrieved.

See Documents Findings example below:

Documents Findings

The third data collection approach was documents. Archival data was retrieved from the ODOE website (ODOE, 2019), where test scores from 2015–2016 through 2019–2020 school years are publicly available. The researcher downloaded the data from the website in the form of an Excel file. According to the ODOE, data that is suppressed has been removed from reports in an effort to protect students' privacy (ODOE, 2019). Such suppression was enacted in reporting assessments results for African American, Hispanic, and Asian student groups, as well as for those of two or more races and English language learners.

Next, present the results in the form of figures and tables. Consider presenting the results in terms of frequency counts, percentages, and/or averages. See the example below.

Table 4. Percent of Students Failing to Meet State Expectations on the OEA for Science at Hampton High School

Year	Overall	Male	Female	Socioeconomically Disadvantaged
2015–2016	51.1	48.5	54.1	70.6
2016–2017	40.9	38.7	43.0	46.7
2017–2018	51.9	62.5	36.4	63.9
Mean	48.0	49.9	44.5	60.4

Also consider using figures to help the readers visualize the data. See the example below.

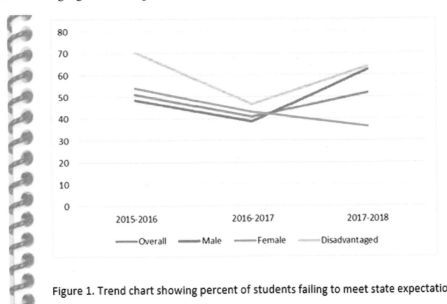

Figure 1. Trend chart showing percent of students failing to meet state expectations on the OEA for Science at Hampton High School.

Graph source: Kurt Michael

Finally, end with a discussion of the findings and any takeaways that emerged from the documents. Use statistics, when appropriate, to support takeaways in the discussion section.

See Documents Discussion of the Findings example below:

Documents Discussion of the Findings

Analysis of the data revealed that there was a sharp increase in the percentage of students failing to meet state expectations on the Ohio Educational Assessment (OEA) for Science at Hampton High School particularly for years 2015–2016 and 2017–2018. Of interest was the number of females passing the assessment showed a steady increase while the males showed a decrease in passing the assessment. By 2017 to 2018 the percent of males' failure to meet state expectation on the OEA for science increased to 62.5% whereas the females decreased to 36.4%. Of the socioeconomically disadvantaged students on average, 60.4% failed to meet the expectations set forth by the state, with the highest percentage occurring during the 2015 to 2016 academic year, in which 70.6% of this population did not meet the expectations. However, the failing percentage among these socioeconomically disadvantaged students decreased to 63% over the three-year time frame. The trend chart (See Figure 1) visually displays an increase in all groups except for a decrease among females. A takeaway for this document analysis is that males and socioeconomically disadvantaged students are at the most risk of not meeting the state's expectations for mastery of the science standards and as a result may warrant special attention.

Checklist for the Documents Findings

- ☐ Does the Document Findings section include the type of documents analyzed?
- ☐ Does the Document Findings section include a brief overview of the procedures?
- ☐ Does the Document Findings section include results in the form of tables and figures?
- ☐ Does the Document Findings section include an interpretation of the data?
- ☐ Does the Document Findings section include a discussion of themes with supporting evidence?
- ☐ The Document Findings section is written in paragraph format.
- ☐ The Document Findings section is written in past tense.

Conclusion

Chapter 7 begins with an introduction to documents and artifacts, which is followed by the procedures for conducting a content analysis. Following the content analysis procedures is a description of how to write the documents procedures and findings. The chapter concludes with a summary of documents and artifacts used in applied research.

Chapter Highlights

A primary source is the original document or artifact under investigation that provides firsthand evidence.

A secondary source is an interpretation of an original document or artifact.

Documents are printed materials in either electronic or hard copy/written form that provides information and/or serves as an official record.

Artifacts are human-made physical objects that have personal, social, or cultural significance.

Content analysis is a method for studying documents or artifacts by counting specific characteristics or attributes embedded in the source material and listing the frequency of occurrence.

The five steps in content analysis are: (1) Collect and organize the date; (2) Look for common attributes, (3) Conduct a frequency count, (4) Make graphs and charts, and (5) Look for trends and patterns in the data.

Attributes are key features or characteristics of an object.

A frequency chart is a table that shows the number of times an event or attribute appears within a data set.

A bar chart is a visual comparison of categorized data plotted by frequency, mean, median, etc.

A trend chart is a chart that displays data over time.

When writing the Procedures and Findings section of an educational report for documents or artifacts, begin each section with an overview.

The Procedures and Findings sections are organized by approach.

CHAPTER 8

Writing the Recommendations for an Educational Report

Objectives

By the end of this chapter, the reader will be able to:

- Describe the process of drafting the Recommendations section of an educational report
- Explain the Roles and Responsibilities of Stakeholders section of an educational report
- Explain the contents of the Resources Needed section of an educational report
- Describe the Timeline section of an educational report
- List the contents of the summary in an educational report

Introduction

The Recommendations section of the educational report is the highlight of the study; it is the culmination of a lot of hard work and dedication to using data to solve a problem of practice to improve education. All the background information, data collection and analysis methods, the literature review, and findings coincide here. The Recommendations section of an educational report includes the researcher's formal recommendations to solve the problem of practice or improve education, the Roles and Responsibilities of Stakeholders, and an explanation of the Resources Needed to complete or carry out the recommendations. The timeline for implementing the recommendations is detailed, and this section closes with a summary of the formal recommendations.

The Recommendations section should begin with an overview of what is covered in the section. The Overview should begin with a brief restatement of the nature and purpose of the study in relationship to the educational site. Then, introduce the reader to the Recommendations. An example of an Overview for the Recommendations section follows.

See Overview example below:

RECOMMENDATIONS

Overview

The purpose of this study was to provide recommendations to the leadership team at Hampton High School with possible solutions to the problem of students' low test scores on the Ohio Educational Assessment (OEA) for Science. In this section, recommendations are presented in an effort to solve the problem of low test scores on the OEA. Additionally, the roles and responsibilities of stakeholders are explained followed by the resources necessary to implement the recommendations and a summary of the recommendations.

Writing the Recommendations

Recommendations

The Recommendations section is where the formal recommendations to solve the problem or improve the practice are disclosed. The recommendations will typically include between one and four specific recommendations, though more may be necessary in rare cases. Below is an example of the beginning of a recommendations section with one of the recommendations listed as a heading.

See Recommendations example below:

Specific Recommendations

The purpose of this study was to provide recommendations to the leadership team at Hampton High School with possible solutions to the problem of students' low test scores on the Ohio Educational Assessment (OEA) for Science. The central research question for this study was, "How can the problem of low test scores on the Ohio Educational Assessment for Science be solved at Hampton High School?" After careful analysis of the data collected in this study, the two most effective solutions recommended to solve the central research question are:

(1) establishing professional learning communities (PLCs) at Hampton High School and

(2) providing targeted professional development to teachers to enhance professional practice.

Recommendation for Professional Learning Communities. Based on the literature, surveys, and interviews, a recommendation to solve this problem of low test scores on the OEA for science is to develop professional learning communities. A professional learning community is a team of teachers who work together to increase student achievement. These communities are deemed effective based on outcomes (DuFour, 2004).

The recommendations section would continue with additional information that is required for the recommendation of professional learning communities. Then, the second recommendation, which is professional development in this example, should be included under a separate heading.

Writing the Recommendations

In this section, begin by restating the purpose of the study. Following the purpose of the study, write the Central Research Question, which should be followed by a list of specific recommendations, listed numerically. Each recommendation should then be listed under a separate heading. For example, if the recommendations to solve the problem are professional learning communities and professional development, then each one of these recommendations should be listed as a separate heading. Here is an example of how the recommendations section should begin:

> The purpose of this study was to provide recommendations to the leadership team at Hampton High School with possible solutions to the problem of students' low test scores on the Ohio Educational Assessment (OEA) for Science. The central research question for this study was, How can the problem of low test scores on the Ohio Educational Assessment for Science be solved at Hampton High School?

The above information should be followed by the specific recommendations made by the researcher that are based on the literature review and data collection and analysis. In the example above, the recommendations are:

(1) establishing professional learning communities (PLCs) at Hampton High School and

(2) providing targeted professional development to teachers to enhance professional practice.

Each proposed solution must include a description of the solution itself, the goals of the solution, a scholarly rationale of why the solution was chosen based on the themes developed in the Findings section (including considerations of the scholarly literature) and a rationale for how the problem will be addressed through the solution. This section must be completed in enough detail so that the proposed solution could be implemented. For example, if the solution to improving co-teaching is three sessions of professional development, then three sessions of professional development must be described in detail. It is not sufficient to simply state that three sessions of professional development on co-teaching will be implemented. Each session should be described in considerable detail using a narrative and outline format. Topics must be presented using evidence from the study (participant quotes, survey results, literature review citations, etc.). Another option is to actually create the professional development sessions. This could be done using PowerPoint. This section should briefly discuss the implications (pros and cons).

Checklist for the Recommendations

☐ Does the Recommendations section include the Purpose of the study?

☐ Does the Recommendations section include the Central Research question?

☐ Does the Recommendations section list specific recommendations numerically?

☐ Does the Recommendations section discuss each recommendation separately using headings?

☐ Does the Recommendations section include justification for each recommendation based on the literature review and data collected?

☐ Does the Recommendations section include the implications (pros and cons)?

 Go to *www.khlearn.com* to watch a video about recommendations.

Roles and Responsibilities of Stakeholders

The Roles and Responsibilities section of your educational report is where detail is provided for the stakeholders. This information should disclose the responsibilities that each person needs to accomplish in order for each recommendation to come to fruition.

See Roles and Responsibilities of Stakeholders example below:

Roles and Responsibilities of Stakeholders

Professional Learning Communities

In order to solve the problem of students' low test scores on the Ohio Educational Assessment (OEA) for Science, it is recommended that professional learning communities be implemented at Hampton High School. Defining the roles and responsibilities of those involved in the professional learning communities is important to ensure success.

Administrators. The role of administrators in professional learning communities would be to determine the purpose and goals, along with the teachers' input. Administration would monitor the overall process and progress of the professional learning communities as a means of ensuring effectiveness. Implementing any new initiative may be met with some skepticism, especially in the case of Hampton High School where interview participants indicated that a flurry of district-based initiatives have come and gone in recent years, many without reaching fruition. As such, teachers may be reluctant to begin the on-boarding process to a new strategy for improving

Writing a Roles and Responsibilities Section

The Roles and Responsibilities section should identify the people needed for each recommendation. List each recommendation as a heading, and then describe the roles and responsibilities of each person needed to accomplish the recommendation. Include possible personnel implications (new hires, training/retraining, certifications, etc.). Describe specific responsibilities assigned to each role. For example: "In order to solve the problem of students' low test scores on the Ohio Educational Assessment (OEA) for Science, professional development is recommended. Professional development would be created by _____ and implemented by _____. Professional development sessions would include all faculty and support staff who would be required to attend all three professional development sessions. This would include _____, and their primary function or functions would be _____." The descriptions in this section should clearly communicate every role and responsibility necessary to successfully implement the recommendation.

Checklist for the Roles and Responsibilities

☐ Does the Roles and Responsibilities section include each recommendation under its own heading?

☐ Does the Roles and Responsibilities section describe the roles and responsibilities of each person needed to accomplish the recommendation?

☐ Does the Roles and Responsibilities section include possible personnel implications (hiring, training, certifications)?

☐ Does the Roles and Responsibilities section describe specific responsibilities assigned to each role?

Resources Needed

The Resources Needed section of your educational report is where the details of resources necessary to implement recommendations are disclosed. These resources may be material or financial.

See Resources Needed example below:

Resources Needed

Professional Learning Communities

It is advisable that teachers have similar schedules beyond that of planning to facilitate shared remediation and enrichment opportunities for students. Ideally, at least two teachers would be teaching the same course, though perhaps at different levels, during the same period. When such a schedule is in place, teachers are able to switch students between classrooms for targeted, homogenous groupings to help students make greater academic gains. In situations where only two teachers are assigned to a course, such as those at the 11th and 12th grade levels, this task may become more challenging, which, again, leads to the suggestion a revision of the course offerings schedule (and thus teachers schedules) to allow for more effective teacher collaboration and to better meet the needs of males and disadvantaged students, and those students who may be struggling with a particular topic. This recommendation requires time to make changes, but there is no financial cost other than time to redistribute course offerings.

Writing the Resources Needed Section

To compose an effective Resources Needed section, the resources needed to accomplish the solution must be described in great detail. Include possible means of procuring the needed resources as well as potential barriers. Numbers should be included that describe, in as much detail as possible, the resources and funds that may be needed to accomplish the recommendations. If multiple recommendations are made, then include a heading for each recommendation. Resources may include funds needed, curriculum, additional faculty and/ or staff, facilities, supplies, technology, etc. Provide enough detail so that all funds needed can be accounted for.

Checklist for the Resources Needed

☐ Does the Resources section include a heading for each of the recommendations?
☐ Does the Resources section include enough detail to account for all resources?
☐ Does the Resources section include numerical values, if applicable?

Timeline

A timeline is necessary so that all stakeholders fully understand the time frame in which the recommendations will be implemented. Each stakeholder, and possibly others, needs to know what they will be expected to do and when they will need to do it. Clearly specifying an accurate timeline will help to ensure that the recommendations are implemented in a timely manner.

See the Timeline example below:

Timeline

Professional Learning Communities

Implementation of the professional learning communities will take approximately eight months. See Table 5 for Timeline of Professional Learning Communities Implementation.

Table 5. Timeline of Professional Learning Communities Implementation

Date	Action Item
January 1, 2021	Introduce the concept of professional learning communities.
February 2, 2021	Science teachers visit another school that currently practices professional learning communities.
February 3, 2021	Teachers share experiences from yesterday's visit.
February 10, 2021	Faculty meeting to discuss the connection between the purpose (including goals and objectives) of the professional learning communities and the mission and vision of the school.
March 1, 2021	Faculty meeting to determine the goals and objectives of the professional learning communities.
March 7, 2021	Continued planning for the professional learning communities. Monthly and yearly goals and objectives should be established in writing.
March 14, 2021	Continued planning for the professional learning communities. More specific detail regarding the monthly and yearly goals and objectives should be written.
April 4, 2021	Determine a timeline for implementation of professional learning communities beginning in the fall of the new school year.
August 19, 2021	One week prior to the first day of school, administrators and

Writing the Timeline Section

The timeline section should specifically disclose when the steps to the recommendations will be carried out and by whom. Dates should be included in this section to communicate when specified benchmarks will be accomplished for each recommendation. Each benchmark should include a date and the person or persons responsible for the benchmark. In some cases, exact dates may be necessary; in other instances, a general time frame, such as summer or fall of this upcoming school year, may be appropriate. The degree of specificity will be determined by the recommendation.

Checklist for the Timeline

☐ Does the Timeline include a timeline for each recommendation in table format?

☐ Does the Timeline include the date and action for completing each item?

☐ Does the Timeline include enough detail that the recommendation could be implemented effectively?

Summary

The Summary section of your educational report is a summary of the research. It should be written concisely and should be about one or two paragraphs long.

See the Summary example below:

Summary

The goal of this study was to identify factors that impact students' performance on the Ohio Educational Assessment for Science at Hampton High School, a suburban high school located in southeastern Ohio. Identifying factors that impacted OEA scores was important since the OEA for Science is one of the publicly available indicators of students' learning. By utilizing data from interviews, an online survey, and a review of documents, it became evident that improvements could be made to help improve students' scores on the OEA for science. This research established the importance of creating professional learning communities and professional development to help increase student's scores on the OEA for Science at Hampton High School.

Writing a Summary Section

Begin the Summary section by stating the goal of the study. Provide a summary of the project. Identify the data collection methods. From the Implications section, reiterate what you consider to be the one or two most important "take-aways" from the results of your research project. Include the specific recommendations to solve the problem or improve the practice.

Checklist for the Summary

☐ Does the Summary include the goal of the study?

☐ Does the Summary include the data collection methods used?

☐ Does the Summary include one or two take-aways from the Implications section?

☐ Does the Summary include the recommendations to solve the problem or improve the practice?

Conclusion

Writing the Recommendations section of an educational report is the culmination of months or even years of work. This section includes an overview of the recommendations to solve the problem of practice or improve practice. The Overview is followed by the specific recommendations made by the researcher. The Roles and Responsibilities for carrying out the recommendations are then described in detail. Resources Needed to implement the recommendations are made, and the resources needed are followed by a detailed Timeline. The timeline specifies dates and duties to be carried out and by whom. Finally, a Summary of the study is written to disclose the recommendations for solving the problem in practice or improving a practice.

Chapter Highlights

The Recommendations section of the educational report is the highlight of the study; it is the culmination of a lot of hard work and dedication to using data to solve a problem of practice to improve education. All the background information, data collection and analysis methods, the literature review, and findings all coincide here.

The Recommendations section is where the formal recommendations to solve the problem or improve the practice are disclosed.

The Roles and Responsibilities section of your educational report is where detail is provided for the stakeholders. This information should disclose the responsibilities that each person needs to accomplish in order for each recommendation to come to fruition.

The Resources Needed section of your educational report is where the details of resources necessary to implement the recommendations are disclosed. These resources may be material or financial.

A timeline is necessary so that all stakeholders fully understand the time frame in which the recommendations will be implemented.

The Summary section of your educational report is a summary of the research. It should be written concisely and should be about one or two paragraphs long.

CHAPTER 9

Example Educational Report

Note: Aspects of the following Educational Report have been changed for the purpose of maintaining anonymity.

 Go to *www.khlearn.com* to watch a video about bringing it all together.

EDUCATIONAL REPORT

Recommendations for Improving Students' Test Scores on the Ohio Educational Assessment for Science at Hampton High School

Prepared for:
Hampton High School
101 Rock Point Road
Columbus, Ohio

Presented by:
Suzanna Brawn

Date:
August 1, 2020

TABLE OF CONTENTS

EXECUTIVE SUMMARY

The problem for this study was that historically, approximately half of the students at Hampton High School failed to meet the state's level of satisfactory performance on the Ohio Educational Assessment (OEA) for Science (Ohio Department of Education [ODOE], n.d.). The purpose of this study was to provide recommendations to the leadership team at Hampton High School with possible solutions to the problem of students' low-test scores on the OEA for Science. Hampton High School is a mid-size suburban public high school in southeastern Ohio. The rationale for this study was that it is critical to implement efforts necessary to raise students' performance on the assessment since improving students' performance on this assessment may ultimately lead to increased funding and programming for the school, boost the community's confidence in the school, improve graduation rates, and prepare students for the future. For this reason, the central research question was, "How can the problem of low test scores on the Ohio Educational Assessment for Science be solved at Hampton High School?" Three forms of data were collected. The first data collection method was interviews with teachers and administrators at Hampton High School familiar with the science assessment. The second form of data collection was a survey administered to all science teachers at the school. The third form of data collection was documents from the ODOE. Data were analyzed and recommendations to solve the problem included establishing professional learning communities (PLCs) and providing professional development to teachers.

ABOUT THE INVESTIGATOR

Suzanna Brawn is a science teacher at Hampton High School. She has been teaching in the Ohio public school system for twelve years. She earned a bachelor's degree from Town College and has a Master of Education degree from State University. She is currently pursuing an Ed.D. in education from West University with a cognate in science education. Suzanna was previously employed as an instructional coach for science  teachers for a school district just outside of Columbus, Ohio. Her instructional coach experience provided her the opportunity to make suggestions to science teachers, science departments, and administrators regarding daily instruction, assessment, and data analysis. As a science teacher at Hampton High School, Suzanna is motivated to improve students test scores on the Ohio Educational Assessment (OEA) for Science. Because she is currently employed by the school within the school's science department, she recognizes that bias and assumptions may have been brought to this study. However, as a researcher, she believes that through a systematic research approach, bias was limited.

PERMISSION TO CONDUCT THE RESEARCH

Permission

Permission was secured from the principal of Hampton High School to conduct the research at the school and to utilize information available regarding the school's performance on the Ohio Educational Assessment (OEA) for Science. See Appendix A for permission letter.

Ethical Considerations

Ethical practices for applied research should be beneficial and should include limited risk to participants; thus, the researcher ensured that, as compared to the benefits of the study, participants did not endure more than minimal risk. Participants were elicited via personal communication. Participants included science teachers and administrators at Hampton High School. Pseudonyms are used to protect the identity of the participants. Interviews were conducted off-campus, which provided an additional level of confidentiality for participants. Identifying information was not collected during the survey process. The documents were collected from a public website. All materials were stored electronically with password protection. These ethical considerations were incorporated into this study to preserve the integrity of the process and results of the study. The information contained in this report is intended to solve a specific problem at a specific location and is not generalizable to a broader population. Therefore, the information will not be shared or distributed outside of Hampton High School. For this reason, Institutional Review Board (IRB) approval was not required.

INTRODUCTION

Overview

The purpose of this study was to provide recommendations to the leadership team at Hampton High School with possible solutions to the problem of students' low test scores on the Ohio Educational Assessment (OEA) for Science. This introduction provides information regarding the organizational profile, an introduction to the problem and its significance, along with the purpose of the study. The central research question is presented, and this section of the report closes with a list of key terms with definitions.

Organizational Profile

The educational site for this study was a suburban public high school in southeastern Ohio. The mission of Hampton High School is to "provide learning opportunities in a safe environment and to help students acquire skills and knowledge necessary to become life-long learners." Hampton High School serves four townships and 859 students. The school is predominantly Caucasian with 7% minority enrollment. Thirty-two percent of the student body is considered economically disadvantaged. A total of 63 teachers serve the school, resulting in a 14:1 student-to-teacher ratio. School administrators include a principal and two assistant principals and a Director of Student Services. For this study, the school's science department was the focus. The science department comprises nine teachers and offers a total of 17 courses. Within the department, leadership is shared among four science teachers who, when responsibilities are combined, function as a department chair. Instructional decisions, including which science courses are taught and the standards associated within these courses, are generally determined among the four science teachers within the department with oversight by an assistant principal.

Introduction to the Problem

The problem is that approximately half of the students at Hampton High School have failed to meet the state's level of satisfactory performance on the Ohio

Educational Assessment (OEA) for Science (ODOE, 2020a). Over the last three academic years, approximately 50% of students failed to meet the ODOE's expectations (ODOE, 2020b). Specifically, low expectations are defined as students' performance that "demonstrates an incomplete understanding of essential concepts in science and inconsistent connections among central ideas" (ODOE, 2018b, p. 14). Students scoring below 50% on the test are considered to have failed the science assessment (ODOE, 2018b). Low scores on the assessment have had a detrimental effect on Hampton High School and have reflected poorly on students, parents, teachers, staff, and administrators, as well as the school board, town governments, and businesses and companies within the region. In the past, the school has tried to solve this problem by requiring teachers to spend more time teaching concepts covered on the test. Most recently, the school has offered free after-school tutoring for students. Both historically and presently, these efforts have not proven effective, as approximately half of the students who take the assessment fail.

Significance of the Problem

The benefits of improving students' performance on the Ohio Educational Assessment (OEA) for Science include extrinsic aspects, such as scholarship and college placement opportunities for students (Ellis, 2018), as well as more intrinsic benefits, including an increased sense of pride and ability. For stakeholders, including teachers and administrators, increased scores on the OEA for Science may lead to increased teacher efficacy, which studies have shown lead to even greater instructional practices (Ware, 2002). An increase in test scores may be seen as a positive indicator on teacher evaluations. Administrators benefit from increased test scores by allowing them to shift their focus on other initiatives within the school, which may lead to increased funding and community support. When students' achievement is high, the school is likely to boast a higher rating among other schools. This can translate to a more desirable community in which to live, increasing property values, attracting businesses and companies, increasing local revenue, employment opportunities, and making the community an ideal location for graduates to live (Lynch, 2015).

Purpose Statement

The purpose of this study is to provide recommendations to the leadership team at Hampton High School with possible solutions to the problem of students' low test scores on the Ohio Educational Assessment (OEA) for Science. This applied research study used both qualitative and quantitative data collection approaches. The first approach used structured interviews with a total of five participants from Hampton High science teachers and one administrator. Each of these participants is familiar with the OEA for Science and students' historical performance on the assessment. The second approach employed a survey of teachers in the science department, two special education collaborative teachers for the science department, the school's testing coordinator and counselor, a retired department chair with 30 years of experience at the school, and four administrators at Hampton High School. This survey was administered using Google Forms, a web-based platform hosted by Google. The third approach utilized a review of documents from the ODOE focusing on Hampton High School students' performance over the last three years on the OEA.

Central Research Question

How can the problem of students' low test scores on the Ohio Educational Assessment for Science be solved at Hampton High School?

Definitions

1. *Accountability* – "the process of evaluating school performance on the basis of student performance measures" (Loeb & Figlio, 2011, para. 1).

2. *Accreditation* – "a process by which recognized authorities validate that an institution meets minimal professional standards and accountability based on its mission" (Greenberg, 2014, p. 2).

3. *Assessment* – "can refer to the process faculty use to grade student course assignments, to standardized testing imposed on institutions as part of increased pressure for external accountability, or to any activity designed to collect

information on the success of a program, course, or University curriculum" (Stassen et al., 2001, p. 5).

4. *Bubble Student* – "students who might otherwise perform just below the proficiency threshold" (Springer, 2008, para. 1).

5. *High-Stakes Testing* – "tests used to make important decisions about students" (Glossary of Education Reform, 2015).

6. *Intervention* – "provide students with support needed to acquire the skills being taught by the educational system and should address functional skills, academic, cognitive, behavioral, and social skills that directly affect the child's ability to access an education" (Lestrund, 2013, para. 1).

7. *Standardized Test* – provides information as to why a child may be struggling or succeeding with specific elements of their grade-level standards; results are used to inform the next step of learning (O'Malley, 2012).

8. *Teacher Effectiveness* – the act of consistently producing higher academic gains among students (Johnson & Semmelroth, 2014).

LITERATURE REVIEW

Overview

The purpose of this study was to provide recommendations to the leadership team at Hampton High School with possible solutions to the problem of students' low test scores on the Ohio Educational Assessment (OEA) for Science. This portion of the report examines literature related to the research problem. The historical significance of standardized testing is discussed, along with its evolution into modern educational practices. Additionally, the OEA for Science is discussed in detail, particularly with regard to how this test was designed and developed, as well as its manner of fulfilling federal accountability requirements. Finally, factors that are associated with students' performance on standardized tests are discussed.

Narrative Review

Standardized Testing

Standardized testing has a long-standing history in American public education. First suggested by Horace Mann in the first half of the 19th century as an alternative to oral exams for students, written examinations were intended to identify the "quality of teaching and learning in urban schools, monitor the quality of instruction, and compare schools and teachers within each school" (Gallagher, 2003, pp. 83–84). Since their introduction, standardized tests have grown in popularity, especially as the population of the United States has grown rapidly through the latter half of the nineteenth century and along with it, the need to provide universal education. These assessments provided educators with information necessary to place students according to ability, rather than the previous practice of grouping students by age (U.S. Congress, Office of Technology Assessment, 1992).

Standardized testing is often tied to the accreditation and accountability policies of school districts as well as the state and federal governments. For instance, in Ohio, students' performance on the Ohio Educational Assessment (OEA) for Science, administered at various times throughout a students' K-12 experience, contribute to a schools' report card by measuring the overall performance of students in English, math, and science (OSAD 75, 2019).

A school's performance on these assessments can determine its accreditation status, which can ultimately impact the availability of funding from various entities. For example, in Ohio, if a school fails to comply with the testing requirements for student participation, funding can be reduced or eliminated. Title I funds, those which are used to support programs that specifically enhance the educational experience of socioeconomically disadvantaged students, can be withheld until reasonable efforts to be compliant with participation standards are made (OSAD 75, 2019). NCLB puts further requirements in place based on standardized testing scores, requiring students to make adequate yearly progress (AYP), and schools that failed to do so are subject to sanctions. These sanctions include developing an improvement plan as a minimum with reconstitution of the school if a school fails to make AYP for 5 years (Lynch, 2016b).

Characteristics of Standardized Tests

Because of accountability requirements in the United States, standardized tests are prominent in every school nationwide. While classroom assessments often include several similarities to standardized tests, a test can only be characterized as standardized if it meets a set of specific criteria. These criteria include being consistent, norm-referenced, criterion-referenced, reliable, and valid (Christensen, 2018). Further, standardized tests follow standard procedures for administration and scoring and include the same content in all versions (Cerezo, n.d.). The consistency of a test can be determined in a number of ways, including test–retest reliability, parallel forms reliability, inter-rater reliability, and internal consistency reliability. Test–retest reliability is "a measure of reliability obtained by administering the same test twice over a period of time to a group of individuals" (Phelan & Wren, 2006, para. 2). Using this method, the reliability of a test is measured by administering the same test to the same group of individuals at two different times and determining the correlation coefficient of the scores (Lavrakas, 2008). Parallel forms reliability is determined by giving two similar tests that measure the same skills and knowledge, but do so with different questions

(Salkind, 2010); comparison of participants' responses provides evidence of the reliability of the test. Inter-relater reliability is best used for tests that require human scoring of answers (Phelan & Wren, 2006). Finally, internal consistency is a useful measure of reliability for tests that probe for the same information with two or more questions on the same test (Frey, 2018). The correlation coefficient between each set of questions is determined, and the reliability is established from this measurement.

Norm-referenced standardized tests compare students' performance on a standardized test to other students of the same age, whereas criterion-referenced assessments compare students' performance to a set of pre-determined skills and standards (Renaissance, 2018). Depending on the assessment's purpose, either one of these references may be appropriate. For example, a criterion-referenced test is an appropriate approach for a driver's test, where a growth chart for children would be an appropriate norm-referenced assessment (Hawker Brownlow Education, n.d.). In education, school-based assessments, such as those at the end of a unit or grading period are prime examples of criterion-based assessments, where more cumulative, large-scale assessments such as the Scholastic Aptitude Test (SAT) are norm-referenced (Glossary of Education Reform, 2015). Both approaches are widely used in standardized assessments.

Due to the accountability requirements of ESSA, state departments of education nationwide have a battery of tests that are required of students at various intervals throughout their K-12 educational experience. These tests are required in math, reading, and science, but states may choose which assessments will be used in their schools that meet the federal requirements. As a result, different states use different tests to measure students' proficiency. Some states choose to use nationally normed tests, such as the SAT and ACT for math and reading, while other states choose to create their own criterion-referenced assessments. Science, despite being required for accountability purposes, is not a required part of school quality reporting (Klein, 2018). Because of this, states have even more freedom in creating their own assessments for science. These tests, while created by different states and each with their own unique qualities, have several shared characteristics. Understanding the similarities and differences between these standardized science tests, as a sample of those administered nationwide on a state-by-state basis, is necessary to fully understand the details and implications of the OEA for Science; as such, each of these tests is discussed in the following sections.

Ohio Educational Assessment for Science

The OEA for Science is part of a battery of tests intended to satisfy the federal requirements for accountability and to inform stakeholders of the progress and proficiency of local schools (ODOE, 2018c). In 1974, the Ohio Assessment of Educational Progress (OAEP) used a series of nationally designed tests to measure a cross-section of 4th- and 8th-grade students in the state. These tests, when compared to national averages, indicated that Ohio students were performing at high levels. This success continued through the 1980s and 1990s, with grades four and eight students in Ohio scoring higher than the national average in math and reading from 1992 until 2000 (Donaldson, 2014).

In the late 1990s, Ohio was considered a leader in educational interests, implementing Ohio's Common Core of Learning (ODOE, 1990) at the start of the decade and Ohio Learning Results in 1997, making the state one of the first to develop state-wide standards for students. Students' progress toward these goals was assessed with OEA, in addition to local districts' self-developed assessments, though local assessments were abandoned in 2007 after concerns about the development of these assessments and their implementation arose (Stone, 2018).

In 2009, the OEA was eliminated in favor of the Ohio Common Assessment Program (OCAP), an assessment used by three other states (Stone, 2018). The change in assessment also meant a change in learning standards; this, combined with the federal Race to the Top initiative to secure more funding, resulted in the adoption of the Common Core Standards and Next Generation Science Standards (NGSS) in 2011 (Stone, 2018). The state adopted the Smarter Balanced assessment for the 2014 to 2015 academic year, along with 18 other states, but this test was only used for 1 year due to rampant objection from students and parents. It was at this time that the SAT became the assessment for math and reading skills for students and the OEA for Science was reinstated (Gallagher, 2015), as there is no SAT component that assesses students' scientific proficiency.

The OEA for Science is administered to students during their third year of high school. Because ESSA dictates that 95% of students in Ohio must take accountability assessments during the specified year (ODOE, 2020b), all students are required to take the test, though no significant penalty is in place for students who do not take the assessment. At Hampton High School, the SAT is given in the spring during the school day rather than on a weekend, which is the traditional SAT administration format (College Board, 2019a), and the OEA for Science is given the day immediately following the administration of the SAT. This is partly in an effort to keep all testing for accountability purposes confined to the same week and under as similar conditions as possible for all students. This, however, increases the likelihood of student burn-out with regard to testing, and inhibits teachers' abilities to review material with students prior to the assessment, which is a common practice with other assessments.

The OEA for Science includes content from both life and physical sciences (ODOE, 2018d), assessed through a series of multiple-choice and constructed response items (ODOE, 2018a). Students will answer 48 multiple-choice questions and five constructed response items, though eight of the multiple-choice questions and one of the constructed response items do not count toward or against students' final scores, as these questions are field-test items (ODOE, 2018a). Each multiple-choice question is worth one point each, while constructed response questions are worth four points each. This gives an overall possible score of 56 points on the assessment. Scores, however, are reported between 1100 and 1180 points. Students must earn at least 1142 out of the 1180 points to meet the state's expectations for performance (ODOE, 2018b).

Similar to other states' science tests, the OEA for Science is required for federal accountability purposes (USDOE, 2016). It is not, however, required for school quality profiles, nor is it a consideration for graduation requirements at Hampton High School

(Hampton High School, 2019). Instead, the data collected from this assessment are used to make comparisons between Ohio students and students in other states, helping stakeholders to assess the quality of Ohio's schools and curriculum and to identify where further supports are needed (ODOE, 2018c).

Strategies to Improve Standardized Test Scores

Because high-stakes standardized testing is prevalent in nearly all public education systems nationwide, bringing with it a myriad of potential benefits and consequences for schools, teachers, and students, it is no surprise that educators seek to identify the factors that have a negative impact on students' performance on standardized assessments. Several factors that have a negative impact on students' performance have been identified including, but not limited to, socioeconomic status, race, child abuse and neglect, and healthy life of individual students (Bertolini et al., 2012). Other factors, however, can have a significantly negative impact on students' achievement, and schools can make changes that help to eliminate these negative influences, sometimes by making changes to current practice and other times by abandoning part of current practice in favor of another strategy that may provide greater gains (Teaching Tolerance, 2019). For instance, analyzing test data, involving parents in their students' education, focusing on bubble students, constant monitoring of success, examining student work, and practice tests and benchmark assessments throughout the academic year can all lead to increased student achievement as measured by a standardized test, such as the OEA for Science (Education World, 2019). Successful implementation of these practices may help increase OEA scores.

Analyzing test data. The first strategy to explore is analyzing test data, which "allows teachers to identify the strengths and weaknesses of an entire class as well as individual students" (National Association of Elementary School Principals, n.d., p. 3). Test data to be analyzed should include all high stakes testing reports and formative and summative assessments within the classroom. By examining this data, teachers begin to develop a sense of how and why students are performing the way they are and can collaboratively plan interventions for each student, whether remediation or extension is needed to meet the student's needs. As more data are collected throughout the year, the data must be analyzed for changes in students' performance, and adjustments must be made to help students to continue to improve.

Parental involvement. Parental involvement in the school community "improves student achievement, reduces absenteeism, and restores parents' confidence in their children's education" (Garcia & Thornton, 2014, para. 5). Students whose families remain actively engaged in the school tend to earn higher grades, perform better on assessments, and exhibit better social skills and classroom behavior. Parental involvement can take many forms, including the active, in-person participation at the school, but it may also include monitoring of online grades and reports, setting goals with children, developing a relationship with teachers, and advocating on behalf of the school to the greater community (Garcia & Thornton, 2014).

Bubble students. Making a concerted effort with bubble students, those who are performing just at or below the threshold for proficiency, can help to boost their scores and the school's overall performance on an assessment by moving these students whose scores are approaching expectations to over the mark. Because these students are close to meeting the criteria, they are likely to benefit from short-term, but intense remediation of missing skills. However, focusing on these students at the exclusion of students who are far below the threshold for success is a dangerous practice since these students could also benefit from remedial efforts. Instead of focusing on one group exclusively, educators would be wise to include all students, even those that are high achieving, moving all students along the continuum of progress so that those close to meeting expectations will, in fact, meet them (Cole, 2008).

Monitoring progress. Monitoring students' progress through the use of benchmark assessments can provide additional indicators as to how students may perform on a high-stakes assessment. Because benchmark assessments are administered periodically, teachers can make note of students' progress toward the end-of-course goal, which may be a high-stakes test, such as the OEA for Science. When these tests are constructed in a way that mimics the structure and rigor of the questions on an assessment such as the OEA for Science, students are likely to perform better on the actual assessment. These benchmark assessments provide information about students' ability to retain information, as the assessments are typically cumulative in nature. Likewise, when authentic questions are used, students become familiar with the format of the test and are more relaxed when they take the high-stakes assessment later on. If constructed properly with clear intentions with regard to the purpose of the test and the users, benchmark assessments are useful for informing instructional practice and policy, as well as decision-making at all levels (Herman et al., 2010).

Instructional practices. One of the most critical steps that educators should take to ensure that students are prepared for high-stakes testing is to ensure that instructional practices are well-aligned to the standards assigned to the course. A common way to accomplish this is by analyzing each standard—"the process of taking the text of each standard and translating it into actual teaching strategies" (WiseWire, 2016, para. 1). By doing this, teachers become aware of the skills and knowledge students must possess in order to be deemed proficient with the standard. Once the skills and knowledge required by students is identified, teachers are better able to match activities and instructional practices to meet students' needs. Another common way that teachers can improve instructional practices is to understand how the standards are vertically aligned from one course to another throughout a student's education (Case, 2005). In the case of the OEA for Science, this is particularly important when examining student's grade 9-11 course sequence, as the standards assessed on the OEA for Science are to be taught during these three academic years. Theoretically, however, this should be happening at all levels, including the elementary and middle school curricula. If, and when, that is done, the district can ensure vertically aligned curriculum, creating a cohesive and thorough science education experience for students, which will aid them in achieving higher scores on high-stakes assessments.

Student Motivation

As noted in previous sections, the OEA for Science is considered a high-stakes standardized tests with regard to its necessity for federal accountability (ODOE, 2018c).

However, because the OEA for Science is not linked to students' grades or graduation requirements, students may not be motivated to put forth their best effort. Additionally, the OEA for Science scores are not used for college admission or scholarship purposes, which may further have a negative impact on student motivation to achieve high scores on the assessment.

Early in their academic career, students tend to be much more motivated and engaged in their education than they are at the end of it (Hulleman & Hulleman, 2018). That is, elementary students tend to have a higher level of motivation to perform well than their high school counterparts. Mathewson (2019) asserts that the reason for students' declining motivation as they progress through their education occurs because of changes in students' excitement about what they are learning. Early on, students are excited to be learning new things, but as they advance, they are required to learn things about which they are not passionate, changing motivation from learning for the sake of learning, an intrinsic motivation, to performing for the sake of earning a grade or credit, an extrinsic motivation (Mathewson, 2019). When a test has a direct consequence or benefit to a student, he or she may be more motivated to perform well than when there are no consequences or benefits based on the outcome of the assessment (Wolf & Smith, 1995). This means that extrinsic motivations can provide more motivation for students to do well, especially at the high school level. The consequences and benefits associated with the OEA for Science, however, are minimal, all but eliminating extrinsic motivation and most certainly reducing intrinsic motivation, as well.

Short of changing graduation requirements and the direct relationship between students' course grades and their performance on the OEA for Science, ways to increase students' motivation lies in the hands of science teachers at Hampton High School. Several practices within the classroom can positively impact students' motivation. These practices include encouraging students to get plenty of rest prior to the test and to engage in stress-reducing activities, setting high expectations, building a culture of success around testing, building positive student-teacher relationships, and positively influencing student mindsets (Martinez, 2018; McKay, 2015). The key, however, to increasing students' motivation on standardized tests is to determine what is causing students to be unmotivated and to then develop a long-term plan of action to motivate students throughout the entire school year (Clay, 2016).

Teacher Effectiveness

Teachers' effectiveness in the classroom has a significant impact on student performance on a variety of assessments, including standardized tests such as the OEA for Science (Darling-Hammond & Youngs, 2002). For this study, the definition provided by Johnson and Semmelroth (2014), that effectiveness is the act of consistently producing higher academic gains among students, will be applied. Though standardized tests can provide a significant amount of data regarding students' academic performance, it cannot and should not be the only source of information in determining a teacher's effectiveness (Piro et al., 2014). In fact, several factors contribute to teachers' effectiveness, including strong content knowledge (DeMonte, 2015), college degrees earned (Stronge, 2018), and teaching credentials obtained by educators (Darling-Hammond, 2015). Professional development, both for new teachers and on-going support for veteran teachers, plays a significant role in teachers' effectiveness (American University, 2018). Further, factors such as the size of the class and the overall size of the school play a critical role in student achievement (Blatchford et al., 2016), as well as teachers' attendance patterns and the qualifications of substitute teachers (Okeke et al., 2015). Determining how these factors contribute to students' scores on the OEA for Science is a critical step in determining how scores can be improved.

The instructional environment at a school is directly linked to the effectiveness of classroom instruction (Heck & Hallinger, 2014). When teachers have an appropriate education, are able to demonstrate content-based competency, and possess teaching credentials required for the course they have been assigned to teach, they are more likely to construct and deliver high-quality lessons for their students (Curry et al., 2018), which may increase students' understanding of skills and concepts measured by the OEA for Science.

Teacher credentials. Studies have indicated that students are more likely to be successful if their teacher possesses a college degree in that area of study rather than a generalized teaching degree (University of Missouri–Columbia, 2018). This is particularly true for high school-level courses since skills and understandings garnered in high school courses are very specific compared to the generalized topics of elementary and middle school. Because of this, the more aligned a teacher's degree is to the content to which they are assigned to teach, the better the academic outcome for their students.

Often, especially at the high school level, teachers are either career-switchers or do not have a formal degree in education. These teachers have a degree in their discipline followed by education courses that meet the requirements for teaching in a public-school system. Many of these teachers have experience in industry prior to teaching; that is, they have used their degree for employment outside of the world of education (Wilcox & Samaras, 2009). Still, others have a degree in a field unrelated to the subject they teach, but they have acquired the credentials necessary to be employed as a teacher. Alternative paths of certification have grown in popularity, as a critical shortage of teachers in certain content areas and in urban settings has remained an issue, along with the high attrition and retirement rate of teachers (USDOE Office of Innovation and Improvement, 2004).

Students whose teachers who have taken an alternative path to licensure are not necessarily at a loss when it comes to the instruction they receive. In fact, the pre-service experiences their teachers have had can greatly enrich their educational experiences in the classroom. The difference, however, lies in the content delivery methods utilized by the teacher. Career switchers often start their teaching careers without a full gamut of education courses, limiting the range of the instructional models with which their teachers may be familiar. As such, instructional delivery can be limited to only a few strategies; targeted interventions may be lacking for students who are struggling to learn content, and enrichment opportunities may be lost for advanced students. The overall instructional planning is often limited for teachers that enter the profession through alternative routes (Lynch, 2016a), and the outcome of poor planning lies in the poor execution of lessons, greatly impacting students' performance on assessments such as the OEA for Science.

Regardless of the method by which teachers enter the profession, all teachers are required to be highly qualified. In order for a teacher to be considered highly qualified, he or she must have earned a bachelor's degree and full state certification, and he or she must prove him or herself competent in the subject which he or she teaches. For middle and high school teachers, competency must be demonstrated via a subject-matter test, a major in the subject or credits equivalent to a major, an advanced certification from the state, or a graduate degree prior to starting their careers. For teachers already in the profession assigned to teach a new subject, additional requirements are necessary and can include prior teaching experience, professional development, and subject-matter knowledge (USDOE, 2004).

Professional development. When a teacher is employed by a school and a district, it is the responsibility of both the school and the district to ensure that professional growth and development occurs throughout the teacher's employment. Professional development is the key to ensuring that best practices are used in the classroom, which can lead to improved scores on standardized assessments, such as the OEA for Science (Fischer et al., 2018). In order for professional development to be effective, however, it must be crafted and encouraged in a way that makes teachers value their experience and seek their own professional development in addition to what is offered at the school, rather than feeling that the development is forced and simply a requirement rather than an opportunity for growth. Developing a culture that supports a growth mindset in a school is imperative to the growth of the individuals within the organization (Dweck, 2000), and because intelligence is malleable, it is critical that the expectations for growth is cultivated. Professional development, whether in-house, workshop-based, online, or full-term courses, helps teachers to stay abreast of current trends in education and empowers them to use a variety of strategies to help their students learn.

Professional development is considered effective if it "is content focused . . . incorporates active learning . . . supports collaboration . . . uses models of effective practice . . . provides coaching and expert support . . . offers feedback and reflection . . . is of sustained duration" (Darling-Hammond et al., 2017, para. 4). Administrators must ensure that professional development is executed in a way that is most beneficial for teachers. This includes a variety of methods that are implemented in a frequent and ongoing manner, focused on both general instructional practices and course- and content-specific practices, intensive and continuous, and monitored for success (Kosanovich & Rodriguez, 2019). Failure to ensure that these considerations are made when developing and implementing professional development can lead to ineffective practice of teachers, resulting in a negative impact on students' scores on assessments such as the OEA for Science.

New teachers. Regardless of the path by which teachers enter the profession, new teachers need support as they become familiar with their new charge. Teaching is no longer simply delivering instruction; rather, teachers must also be well-versed in mediation, discipline, customer service, documentation, differentiation, accommodation, data analysis, committee work, technology, and a seemingly endless list of other duties that are otherwise undefined in most job descriptions. Learning how to manage these responsibilities, on top of the expectation to provide an education to students, linking prior knowledge to new material in an effort to prepare them for their futures, is difficult for even the best and most prepared teachers. A purposeful new teacher support program can be the key to minimizing the stress caused by these responsibilities, helping teachers to build efficacy and competency, while minimizing the burnout that is often experienced by teachers, overwhelmed as they enter the profession (Ingersoll, 2012). In fact, research has shown that new teacher support programs, or new teacher induction programs, can be the key in retaining high-quality teachers. New teachers that received no support as they entered the profession have a predicted turnover rate of 41%, while those with basic support, which includes mentoring and a supportive administrator, have a 39% probability of turnover, and those who participated in a more comprehensive support program have a predicted turnover rate of 18% (Johnson et al., 2005, as cited in Solomon, 2016). Additionally, new teacher support programs not only help to improve retention rates, but such programs have also resulted in a marked improvement in the quality of instructional practices used by new teachers (California County Superintendents Educational Services Association, 2016); transferring skills learned during teachers' college experiences can be challenging without the support structures of a formal induction program (Kielwitz, 2014). The combination of teacher retention and the use of high-quality instructional methods often produces higher levels of student achievement (California County Superintendents Educational Services Association, 2016).

New teacher support programs come in a variety of shapes and sizes, as well as differences in which teachers are invited to participate. While it is critical that each program matches the school, district, and teachers that it intended to serve, there are common characteristics that should be shared among all programs. The ODOE has set forth standards by which induction programs in the state must abide (ODOE, 2002). From these standards, recommendations as to what components induction programs should contain were developed. These recommendations include a new teacher orientation that provides pertinent information about the school and district, mentoring relationships that can involve observation and collaborative teaching and planning, support teams upon which new teachers can rely, workshops specifically targeted the needs and concerns of new teachers, and evaluation so that new teachers can develop self-reflection skills in their efforts to grow as professionals as outlined by expectations, standards, and processes (ODOE, 2002). According to Huling-Austin (1990, as cited in Stansbury & Zimmerman, 2000), the goal of such programs is improving teacher performance, increasing the retention of promising beginning teachers, promoting the personal and professional well-being of beginning teachers, satisfying mandated requirements for induction and/or licensure, and transmitting the culture of the system to beginning teachers.

One of the most notable induction programs is the New Teacher Center (NTC) based in California. The NTC is a non-profit organization that strives to provide support structures and resources to schools and new teachers to help improve instructional practices in four key areas: "student learning, educator effectiveness, leadership development, and optimal learning environments" (NTC, 2019, para. 2). The organization focuses on cycles of support, during which observations are conducted and feedback is provided to new teachers by a mentor teacher that has received training from the organization. These observations are available in an online portal (NTC, 2016c) and include selective scripting, seating chart: movement, interaction, and behavior patterns, and content, strategies, and alignment (NTC, 2016b). Additionally, forms and protocols are available for new teachers who focus on analyzing student work, lesson plans, and parent communication (NTC, 2016a). The NTC recommends that all new teachers participate in an induction program for the first two to three years of their careers at a minimum (Jacobson, 2018). Other programs, such as Greenville Public School District in Mississippi, recommend 3 to 4 years of support, with the expectations and experiences changing from year-to-year based on teachers' individual development (Greenville Public School District, n.d.).

While full-fledged induction programs are not feasible in all situations, all programs should, at a minimum, include a mentoring component. Mentors should be paired intentionally, using the best teachers to help guide new teachers as they navigate their first year. These pairings can be determined by proximity of classrooms, similarity in content, and commonality in educational background, among other characteristics. However, according to Steelman (2018), the best partnerships result when the mentor and mentee teach at least one common course. This allows the partnership to focus on instructional strategies and classroom management techniques, both in general and for specific lessons. Mentoring relationships also thrive when partners are able to meet frequently, are reflective, and encourage positivity, despite the vulnerability of such a relationship (Steelman, 2018). Teachers that feel supported are more likely to remain in the field, and studies have shown that these programs help to greatly reduce the attrition rate of new teachers, which can be as high as 40% to 50% (Ingersoll & Strong, 2011). Because the correlation between new teacher support programs, teacher retention, and student performance is strong, it is necessary to determine the level to which teachers at Hampton High School feel supported, not only currently, but also the level of support that they received upon starting at the school in order to solve the problem of low assessment scores on the OEA for Science.

Class and school size. The size of the class in which students are enrolled can have a direct impact on the instructional experience students have. When relationships between students and teachers flourish, opportunities for remedial and enrichment opportunities become available, behavioral challenges subside, and student engagement increases (Higgins, 2014). Unfortunately, staffing is limited in many schools due to budget constraints, causing class sizes to grow and students' learning and academic achievement to be compromised, as measured in a number of ways, including standardized assessments such as the OEA for Science.

Students' perceptions and sense of belonging within a classroom can be a determining factor of their academic achievement. When meaningful relationships exist between students and their teachers, students are more likely to want to please their teacher, resulting in improved behavior (Boynton & Boynton, 2005) and a likeliness to engage in challenging activities that are outside of their comfort zones (Thompson, 1998). Students feel more confident taking risks when trying new skills and activities, while being more engaged in their learning, out of a desire to please their teacher and avoid negative interactions (Thijs & Fleischmann, 2015). Because of this, students are more likely to deepen their understandings, which can translate to higher assessment scores.

In schools where student-to-teacher ratios are small, students are more likely to receive one-on-one instruction, which can benefit struggling learners as they receive remedial support, as well as high-achieving students who engage in enrichment activities (Cuseo, 2007). These individual interactions with the teacher provide the opportunity for relationships to develop between students and the teacher; positive relationships can foster an intrinsic motivation in students that develops from the extrinsic motivation to impress the teacher (Kalenze, 2016). Therefore, positive relationships between teachers and students, when given the time to develop and be cultivated, can increase students' achievement; determining the extent to which teachers feel relationships exist at Hampton High School informed the recommendations for improving the scores on the OEA for Science at the school.

Students' behavior and level of engagement both tend to improve in smaller classes (Finn et al., 2003). This decrease of behaviors that take away from students' learning and the increase in student engagement allows students to better interact and understand new learning. Further, research has shown that students in smaller classes can be as many as two months ahead of their peers that are in larger classes (National Council of Teachers of English, 2014); these same students were shown to perform better on assessments. However, Osborne (2018) cautioned against putting too much stock in the impact of smaller class sizes on performance, as studies of the impact of smaller class size on achievement by both Hoxby (1998) and Chingos (2010) show that smaller class sizes do not necessarily correlate to better performance on standardized assessments.

Teachers with small class sizes are more likely to feel less overwhelmed by their teaching responsibilities, spending less time grading for the sake of grading and devoting more time to offering meaningful and growth-minded feedback to students (EF Academy, 2019). Meaningful and timely feedback provides students with information as to whether or not they are appropriately learning the new skill or task at hand; in order to be effective, however, it must be as specific as possible, given immediately, address the student's work toward a specific goal, be presented purposefully, and involve the student (Stenger, 2014). In addition to providing the opportunity for teachers to provide this sort of feedback, smaller class sizes also foster a community in which students are open to receiving feedback from their peers, and the management of this process is much more successful with smaller groups of students rather than larger groups. This feedback can help students grow in their academic achievement as measured by a variety of indicators, including the OEA for Science.

Small class sizes can also lead to an increase in teacher effectiveness and efficacy because teachers are better able to form relationships with their students. Logically, the fewer students' teachers have in their classroom, the more one-on-one time they can effectively spend with each student, fostering a relationship that empowers students to challenge themselves academically (Thijs & Fleischmann, 2015). These relationships are able to bolster students' confidence when it is waning in the face of an obstacle and are part of the celebration when students find success. When these correlations are recognized by teachers, their own confidence soars and enthusiasm for teaching climbs, both of which translate to better instruction and better academic achievement for students (Ware, 2002).

Teacher attendance. Just as students' attendance is imperative to their success at school, so is a teacher's attendance necessary for student's success. When teacher absences occur frequently, students' learning is disrupted, and their overall academic performance is at risk. Most notably, when teachers are absent in the weeks and months immediately prior to high stakes testing, students' scores tend to suffer considerably. Though substitute teachers are hired in the absence of a full-time educator, lessons are far less effective with a substitute teacher present than when the regular classroom teacher is in attendance (Okeke et al., 2015).

Research currently demonstrates that teacher absenteeism does, in fact, have a negative impact on students' performance and student achievement. In fact, Miller et al. (2007) found that as few as 10 teacher absences can have a detrimental effect on students' performance on standardized assessments; what is alarming about this finding is that each teacher misses an average of 10 school days per academic year. Though these 10 days do not necessarily occur consecutively, the impact it has on student learning often exceeds a 10-day deficit (Whelan, 2008). While some studies, such as that of Ehrenberg and Brewer (1995) noted that teachers' attendance did not have a considerable impact on students' test scores, other studies have noted the significantly negative impact teachers' absenteeism has on students' assessment performance (Aucejo & Romano, 2016; Pianta & Ansari, 2018). Because of the conflicting findings in these prior studies, the current study is warranted to determine the impact of teachers' attendance patterns on students' performance on the OEA for Science at Hampton High School.

Substitute teacher qualifications. When teachers are absent, substitute teachers are typically hired on a day-by-day basis to ensure that students continue to receive their regular classroom education. While the intentions of this practice are sound, several issues lie within the hiring of substitute teachers. These issues generally lie in the lack of qualifications of substitute teachers due to inexperience with both content and classroom management techniques. In a study by Westrick et al. (2015), it was found that students are more likely to exhibit challenging behaviors when a substitute teacher is present than when their regular classroom teacher is in attendance. This is partly due to the change in the daily routine, the lesson plans provided, which often incorporate less-engaging activities, and a lack of connection to the substitute teacher in a way that mimics the relationship between the regular classroom teacher and students (Davies, 2019). Because a substitute teacher is usually employed one day at a time, he or she is less likely to form these relationships, ones that would otherwise lead to an understanding of students' academic needs in a way that can help them to be successful. This, in turn, can have a negative impact on students' learning and their later performance on standardized assessments, such as the OEA for Science.

Perhaps the biggest concern with substitute teachers is that they seldom have the full teaching credentials that regular classroom educators are required to possess. Though some substitute teachers are retired full-time educators or individuals with full teaching credentials, many possess the minimum qualifications necessary. In Ohio, a substitute teacher can be employed up to 10 days in any position with only a General Education Diploma (GED) or high school diploma (National Education Association, 2019b). A more alarming detail of the substitute policy in Ohio is the trend for schools to hire substitute teachers who fail to possess the appropriate content knowledge and classroom skills as long-term substitutes for various vacancies (National Education Association, 2019a). Add to this detail the fact that schools do not need to notify parents and guardians of the hiring of an underqualified teacher for a position per the NCLB Act (2001), as the substitute is not hired as a full-time teacher, and students' success becomes even more at risk, as parents are unaware of the need to advocate for their children differently than if a full-time teacher were hired.

Instructional Resources

The instructional resources available for use in the classroom can strongly support students' learning in the science classroom. Textbooks, electronic resources, and consumables for hands-on learning, among other tools, are available for teachers to use in their classrooms, but without the assurance that these resources are closely aligned with the content, rigor, and abilities of students in the classroom, these tools can be ineffective (Matthews, 2012). However, when classroom instructional resources are appropriate, the resources can have as significant of an impact on students' learning as would reducing class size by 10 students (Koedel & Polikoff, 2017). While factors that should be considered when selecting appropriate resources for classroom instructional purposes vary from district to district, many similarities exist between selection criteria. These include supporting the goals and objectives of the course, school, and district, be appropriately matched to students' age, social, and emotional development, and offer diverse applications in terms of difficulty, appeal, and points of view (Urbandale Community School District, 2019). In order to understand if and how resources are matched to the goals of the course, school, and district, individuals tasked with choosing resources, whether as a committee on behalf of a larger group or individual teachers selecting tools for their classrooms, a thorough understanding of the underlying beliefs of the school and district must be present in order to ensure that resources are not misaligned. Likewise, a deep knowledge and understanding of all course standards and the way in which these standards are interwoven throughout the course will help to ensure appropriate materials are selected. While textbooks have been the long-standing choice as the primary instructional resource, a variety of options now exist, available from both from publishing companies and in piecewise format with a careful search by educators. These resources can include the textbooks, along with workbooks, worksheets, and manipulatives, such as flash cards, games, models, and activities, to help support classroom instruction. Electronic resources are also available in a variety of formats, including apps, websites, movies, podcasts, and online activities. These tools can be used in several different combinations to best meet the learning needs of students.

Summary

This literature review provided the history of standardized testing, the structure of standardized tests, the use of standardized testing in science nationwide, the history and evolution of the Ohio Educational Assessment (OEA) for Science testing process, including the use of the OEA for Science, underlying factors that impact students' performance on assessments, and strategies and interventions that can improve student achievement as measured by standardized tests. These strategies include analyzing test data, involving parents in their students' education, focusing on bubble students, constant monitoring of success, examining student work, and practice tests and benchmark assessments throughout the academic year, as well as unpacking standards and ensuring a vertically aligned curriculum. The literature review revealed that strategies exist that can improve student performance on standardized assessments, which serve as one of several indicators of students' proficiency as related to standards. This then beckons the question, what strategies and interventions can be implemented at Hampton High School to improve students' performance on the OEA for Science? More research is necessary to determine what strategies are already in place and which ones would most benefit students in both the short- and long-term applications. The literature emphasizes the importance of research in this area; therefore, this applied research study sought to contribute to the field of knowledge in the research and literature concerning the strategies that can best aid students and teachers in achieving higher scores on standardized science assessments, such as the OEA for Science.

PROCEDURES

Overview

The purpose of this study was to provide recommendations to the leadership team at Hampton High School with possible solutions to the problem of students' low test scores on the Ohio Educational Assessment (OEA) for Science. Hampton High School is a mid-size suburban public high school in southeastern Ohio. This portion of the report provides interview procedures, survey procedures, and documents procedures.

Interviews Procedures

The first approach used to collect data in this study was semi-structured interviews. This approach allowed the researcher to construct interview questions based on specific topics to be investigated, and it allowed the researcher to format questions in a way that incorporated previous answers based on each participant's experiences. Conducting interviews allowed the researcher to determine how teachers and administrators would solve the problem of low scores on the Ohio Educational Assessment (OEA) for Science at Hampton High School located in southeastern Ohio. Purposeful sampling was used to elicit participants (Bickman & Rog, 2009). The five faculty members consisted of one administrator, two 9th grade teachers, and three 11th grade teachers. The participants were selected based on their historical familiarity with the OEA for Science and the assessment results for Hampton High School.

The interviews were conducted off-campus in a one-on-one, face-to-face format. Standard interview protocol was utilized during the interviews (Creswell, 2015). Each interview lasted approximately one hour and was recorded and immediately transcribed for data analysis. Throughout the interview, the researcher made note of body language and tone during the interviews to further define the participants' thoughts and feelings toward each topic included in the interview. After participants consented to participate in the study, the 16 questions below were utilized for the interviews.

Once interviews were transcribed, the transcripts were reviewed, and coding was used to determine the categories and themes present in the participants' dialogue.

Coding and categorization were appropriate data analysis methods as they allowed the researcher to align the participants' responses with the literature related to the study (Creswell & Poth, 2018). This data analysis method also lends itself to the creation of a table of codes, from which the researcher determined what constitutes an entry under a specific theme along with what does not (Creswell & Poth, 2018). Generally speaking, coding involves reading the transcript from each interview and identifying the various themes that are represented throughout. To answer the central research question, data were collected in a qualitative manner via 16 semi-structured questions. After participants consented to participate in the study, the following 16 questions were utilized for the interviews.

Interview Questions

1. What skills are assessed with the OEA for Science?

This question aimed to determine educators' awareness of how the OEA for Science is aligned with Next Generation Science Standards (NGSS). Understanding the alignment of an assessment with standards in terms of rigor and content is critical to ensuring the assessment accurately measures students' abilities with the material and skills (Carnegie Mellon University, 2019). By asking this question, the researcher will learn how familiar teachers are with which skills and concepts are assessed on the OEA.

2. How are these skills incorporated through students' 9-12 curriculum map?

This question aimed to determine educators' familiarity with the standards included on the OEA for Science and how they are incorporated into the science course offerings at Hampton High School. Ensuring that all concepts to be assessed are taught at an appropriate rigor level throughout the courses that all students are required to take is necessary to provide students the academic experiences necessary to be successful on the test (Drake & Burns, 2004). Likewise, understanding the vertical alignment of science course offerings at Hampton High School may create a cohesive experience for students prior to taking the assessment (Case, 2005).

3. How do the day-to-day instructional strategies in your classroom prepare students for the assessment?

The purpose of this question was to uncover the extent to which teachers work to teach standards within their course. Teaching the standards helps to ensure that the instructional practices are aligned with both the content and the rigor required of the standards (Wiggins & McTighe, 2005).

4. How do the instructional resources available, including textbooks and other in-class materials, as well as electronic tools, support daily instructional practices?

This question was intended to determine the extent to which the current instructional materials support daily instruction. Appropriately aligned resources are imperative for student success, but the resources must be aligned to the course content, rigor of the standards, and abilities of the students in class (Koedel & Polikoff, 2017).

5. How do students demonstrate mastery of these skills and concepts in your class?

The purpose of this question was to uncover how formative and summative assessments are used in each science course. The use of such assessments can serve as a predictor of students' performance on high-stakes assessments such as the OEA for Science (Herman et al., 2010). When assessments are used in a formative manner, teachers are able to offer interventions to students to improve their learning (William, 2018), which is measured by the OEA for Science.

6. The OEA is administered during a student's 11th grade year of high school and is a cumulative exam. How are skills needed to be successful on the OEA learned during the 9th and 10th grade years reflected in the curriculum map?

This question was designed to determine what review strategies, if any, are used with students to help them prepare for the OEA for Science. A review of content can help to reduce test anxiety, help students gain confidence, and help students study more effectively (Nest, 2019).

7. What specific test preparation is offered to students prior to taking the OEA?

This question seeks to determine what review strategies, if any, are used with students to help them prepare for the OEA for Science. A review of content can help to reduce test anxiety, help students gain confidence, and help student's study more effectively (Nest, 2019). It also helps students call to mind information that was learned in prior courses.

8. For the past three years, Hampton High School students have scored in the bottom half (and sometimes the bottom quarter) of all schools in the state. What factors do you believe contribute to such low test scores?

This question called for educators to consider what factors might negatively impact students' performance on the OEA for Science. While some of these factors are beyond the control of the school, several may be addressed by making small adjustments to instructional practices and mindsets (Teaching Tolerance, 2019).

9. When the assessment results are shared with the department, what do you think should be the next steps for teachers?

This question aimed to identify ways that teachers have used the test data to make instructional decisions. When teachers work collaboratively to analyze test data, they can better understand the strengths and weaknesses of students overall, which can lead to an adjustment in instructional practices to help improve students' performance future (National Association of Elementary School Principals, n.d.).

10. What strategies have been explored to increase students' performance on the test?

This question sought to identify what strategies have been considered in the past to improve students' performance on the OEA for Science and why they were or were not chosen for implementation. Several strategies exist (Teaching Tolerance, 2019), but not all strategies are the correct fit for all students, making the selection of strategies a critical practice to ensure students' learning needs are being met.

11. How were these strategies decided upon?

The purpose of this question was to determine if and how teachers work together to make instructional decisions, whether by content or as a department as a whole. Working collaboratively provides teachers the opportunity to further enhance their practice and increase student performance (DuFour, 2004).

12. How were they implemented?

This question also sought to identify whether work is completed independently or collaboratively among teachers and with what fidelity. It is not enough to simply choose appropriate interventions for students to improve their learning and, therefore, their test score; educators must make sure that the strategies are implemented in a way that is effective (National Center on Response to Intervention, n.d.).

13. How do you think students feel about taking this assessment and what evidence do you have to support your opinion?

This question was intended to collect data regarding educators' perceptions of students' motivation to perform well on the OEA for Science. Because the OEA for Science is not directly linked to any consequence, whether positive or negative, for students, they may not be motivated to do well (Wolf & Smith, 1995). Further, this question sought educators' perceptions of how students' motivation impacts their performance on the assessment. Students that are motivated would likely be disappointed by their poor performance, but if students are not motivated to do well on the assessment, they will likely be indifferent toward their scores (Tyner, 2018).

14. In what ways do you feel that teacher effectiveness impacts students' performance on the OEA for Science?

This question allowed participants to reflect on their practice, as well as that of their peers, with regard to students' performance on the OEA for Science. Such reflection may reveal what characteristics each participant feels define effective instruction, as well as what can be immediately changed to improve instruction (Sierra, 2015). Reflective practice, defining expectations, and desirable qualities in teachers is critical to the growth of an individual and the growth of the science department as a whole, which translates to better instruction for students and possibly higher scores on the OEA for Science.

15. What factors positively impact students' performance on this test?

This question allowed educators to communicate what they feel is working well at Hampton High School with regard to students' performance on the OEA for Science. These are likely to be things that will remain unchanged in the future and bringing to light the positive components already in place is key to improving the areas in which instructional practices and student performance are falling short. These successes should be celebrated and maintained as the more challenging work of changing factors that have a negative impact on students' performance begins (Battelle for Kids, 2011).

16. What other thoughts or feedback about how students' scores on the OEA could be increased at our school could you add?

This final question allowed participants to provide any other thoughts that they have about the OEA for Science and why they believe scores are as low as they are. Using this open-ended format for this question allows for "richer and more extensive" data to be collected than close-ended questions (Bickman & Rog, p. 264).

Survey Procedures

The second approach used to collect data in this study was a survey. This approach explored how science educators participating in a survey would solve the problem of low test scores on the Ohio Educational Assessment (OEA) for Science at a suburban public high school in southeastern Ohio. To collect data, a closed ended Likert scale survey was administered electronically using Survey Monkey, an internet-based program. A quantitative survey is an appropriate approach for data collection for this study since it provides participants with the opportunity to have one and only one answer to each question, while ensuring that there is, in fact, an answer to every question (Bickman & Rog, 2009).

Participants included 13 teachers, one special education teacher, and two administrators at Hampton High. This was a purposeful sample because of the participants' familiarity with the science program (Creswell & Poth, 2019). The participants received an email with instructions regarding how to complete the survey. The email included the link to Survey Monkey, consent to participate, and instructions on how to complete the survey. The participants were given a two-week time frame in which to complete the survey; if more time was needed, arrangements were made. The results were analyzed by calculating the frequency of each number reported on the Likert scale on a question-by-question basis, as well as the average score reported by all participants for each question. The survey included demographic questions and 15 statements developed from the literature review, to which survey participants responded using a 5-point Likert scale rating. The prompts on the survey included the following questions.

Demographic Questions

1. Which category best describes your age in years?

    21–29

    30–39

    40–49

    50–59

    60 or older

2. What is your race?

    White

    Black/African-American

    Asian

    Native American/Pacific Islander

    Two or More Races

    Other

3. What is your gender?

    Male

    Female

4. What is the highest educational degree you have received?

    Less than High School Diploma or Equivalent (GED)

    High School Diploma or Equivalent (GED)

    Associate Degree

    Bachelor's Degree

    Graduate Degree

    Doctorate

5. What grades do you teach? (You may select more than one).

    9th grade

    10th grade

    11th grade

    12th grade

Survey Questions

1. Classroom instruction is delivered with the same rigor specified in the NGSS standards.

5	4	3	2	1
Always	Often	Sometimes	Rarely	Never

This question sought to identify how well-aligned instruction is with the standards and the rigor of each. Ensuring that students are learning material, albeit scaffolded at the onset, at the same level at which they are expected to demonstrate mastery, leads to better standardized test performance (Drake & Burns, 2004).

2. Time is provided during contract hours for collaboration between teachers of the same courses.

5	4	3	2	1
Always	Often	Sometimes	Rarely	Never

Meeting with other teachers of the same course helps teachers to disaggregate data and provide insight into students' performance. This question was intended to identify the frequency of these meetings that occur during contract hours, when teachers are most likely to analyze data effectively and complete the task. Further, during this time, instructional decisions can be made, and the collaborative planning that occurs during these meetings can lead to improved lessons for all teachers (DuFour, 2004).

3. Data collected from assessments are used to plan future instruction.

5	4	3	2	1
Always	Often	Sometimes	Rarely	Never

This question helped to determine the manner in which assessment data are used to plan instruction. When formative, as well as summative, assessments are used to determine students' understanding of concepts, instruction can be tailored to students' needs, increasing performance on standardized assessments (William, 2018).

4. Content taught in each course is clearly communicated throughout the department.

5	4	3	2	1
Always	Often	Sometimes	Rarely	Never

This question sought to identify the level of vertical alignment within the science department at Hampton High School. Vertical alignment within the department ensures that time is allocated in an appropriate manner to each standard throughout a student's science progression. When too much or too little time is spent on a concept depending on a students' prior knowledge of the material, performance on assessments can be negatively impacted. Understanding how and when concepts are taught throughout the science sequence at Hampton High School creates a comprehensive educational experience for students, which may improve their performance on the OEA for Science (Case, 2005).

5. Professional development focuses on new instructional strategies has been offered to science teachers.

5	4	3	2	1
Always	Often	Sometimes	Rarely	Never

This question was intended to pinpoint the frequency of introduction of new instructional strategies for teachers. While a number of options exist for instructional methods, it is important that teachers are well-versed in a variety of approaches, including those that are less common in the district, as well as those that are new to the world of education (Fischer et al., 2018).

6. Students are ready to learn in my class each day.

5	4	3	2	1
Always	Often	Sometimes	Rarely	Never

Students' motivation can be highly influential on their performance on a standardized assessment (Wolf & Smith, 1995). As such, when students are excited to learn and engage in class, they are more likely to perform better on standardized assessments. This question sought to identify the level of excitement, as perceived by teachers, of students at Hampton High School.

7. Teachers regularly participate in meaningful data analysis conversations.

5	4	3	2	1
Strongly Agree	Agree	Neither Agree nor Disagree	Disagree	Strongly Disagree

This question sought to identify the level of engagement between teachers specifically related to data analysis. When teachers discuss the data gathered from common lessons and assessments, the conversations can provide insight as to what instructional strategies have been effective, allowing teachers to learn from one another in an effort to improve their own practice (DuFour, 2004). This collaborative aspect of teacher interaction may improve the instructional quality of courses, leading to improved test scores on standardized assessments.

8. The science department at Hampton High School is made of teachers that are highly qualified educators.

5	4	3	2	1
Strongly Agree	Agree	Neither Agree nor Disagree	Disagree	Strongly Disagree

This question was intended to determine the overall quality of the science department at Hampton High School. When teachers are highly qualified, the quality of their instructional practices is better, leading to better student achievement (Darling-Hammond, 2015).

9. On-going support is provided to new teachers.

5	4	3	2	1
Strongly Agree	Agree	Neither Agree nor Disagree	Disagree	Strongly Disagree

When new teachers are part of an on-going induction program, they are more likely to remain in the profession, improve their practice, and have higher-achieving students (Ingersoll, 2012), thus this question sought to identify whether or not teachers believe that new teachers are provided with on-going support.

10. Professional development that serves the instructional needs of teachers is provided.

5	4	3	2	1
Strongly Agree	Agree	Neither Agree nor Disagree	Disagree	Strongly Disagree

This question was intended to pinpoint the alignment of professional development with the efforts of teachers in the science department at Hampton High School. Responsive professional development can help to build teachers' effectiveness by delivering timely and targeted training to build their skillset and improve instructional practices (American University, 2018).

11. Teachers in the science department at Hampton High School have high attendance rates.

5	4	3	2	1
Strongly Agree	Agree	Neither Agree nor Disagree	Disagree	Strongly Disagree

This question sought to determine the attendance rate of teachers within the science Department of Hampton High School. When teachers frequently miss school, the achievement of students is severely compromised (Okeke et al., 2015).

12. When teachers are absent from school, high-quality substitute teachers are hired.

5	4	3	2	1
Strongly Agree	Agree	Neither Agree nor Disagree	Disagree	Strongly Disagree

This question was intended to determine the perceived quality of the substitutes hired at Hampton High School should a teacher need to be absent. When substitutes are not well-qualified, the instructional component of a substitute lesson plan is often compromised, having a negative impact on student achievement (Davies, 2019).

13. Class sizes in the science department at Hampton High School are conducive to student learning.

5	4	3	2	1
Strongly Agree	Agree	Neither Agree nor Disagree	Disagree	Strongly Disagree

This final question sought to identify teachers' perceptions of the appropriateness of class sizes as it relates to student learning. When class sizes are small, students are more likely to have positive experiences and increased performance on a variety of assessments (Cuseo, 2007).

Documents Procedures

The third approach used to collect data for this study was document analysis. This approach explored how a review of documents could inform the problem of low test scores on the Ohio Educational Assessment (OEA) for Science. A document is printed material in either electronic or hard copied written format that provides information and/or serves as an official record (Bickman & Rog, 2009). Archival data was retrieved from the ODOE website (ODOE, 2019). The site was used because it provided school data including test scores from the 2015–2016 school years through 2019–2020. This review of documents produced quantitative results and is important because it provides evidence of students' historical performance on the OEA for Science. The information is available to the public. Data gathered from this approach is presented in tabular format and as a trend chart.

FINDINGS

Overview

The purpose of this study was to provide recommendations to the leadership team at Hampton High School with possible solutions to the problem of low test scores on the Ohio Educational Assessment (OEA) for Science. This section of the report includes interview findings, survey findings, and documents findings.

Interview Findings

The first approach used in this study was interviews. Semi-structured interviews consisting of 16 questions were conducted with each participant on an individual basis. The purpose of these interviews was to focus on the factors that impact the low test scores on the Ohio Educational Assessment (OEA) for Science at Hampton High School. Interviews were conducted off-site, either at the local public library or at a restaurant. A total of five participants took part in the fact-to-face interviews. The participant criteria for interviews were a tenure of 3 years or more at Hampton High School and a familiarity with the OEA for Science. Because of their tenure at the school, these participants have been directly involved in science instruction, analysis of the OEA scores, or both. Prior to beginning each interview, participants were provided with a brief summary of the purpose of the study in addition to the information they received when invited to participate in the study. Each interview lasted approximately 1 hour and were recorded and immediately transcribed for data analysis. Throughout the interview, the researcher made note of body language and tone demonstrated during the interviews to further define the participants' thoughts and feelings toward each topic included in the interview.

Interview Descriptions of Participants

The first interview candidate was Mrs. Harrison, the building principal, with 29 years of experience in education, eight of which were spent as an administrator at Hampton High School. Prior to entering administration, she was an elementary teacher, teaching both math and English, and her administrative experience started at the middle school level. Because of her experiences at all three levels of education, Mrs. Harrison brought a unique and interesting perspective to the study.

Mr. Gilmer is currently in his second year as a co-department chair and has been teaching at Hampton High School for 15 years, with 3 years as a teacher elsewhere prior. While he teaches mostly 12th grade students who have already taken the Ohio Educational Assessment (OEA) for Science prior to enrolling in his course, Mr. Gilmer's leadership within the science department, as well as his keen eye for data analysis, has resulted in a strong familiarity with the OEA for Science and its results at Hampton High School, along with experience discussing these results with others.

Mrs. Smith is the other co-department chair and has been a science teacher for 13 years, all of which have been spent at Hampton High School. Historically, Mrs. Smith has taught 9th grade science and biology, both of which are courses that students enroll in prior to their junior year, during which they take the OEA for Science.

Mr. Preston is in his fourth year as a science teacher at Hampton High School, with 6 years a science teacher elsewhere. Mr. Preston's current teaching assignment includes only a small number of 11th grade students that will be taking the OEA while they are enrolled in his class; most others are seniors and have taken the test prior to being in one of Mr. Preston's classes. Prior to his current assignment, he taught 9th grade science at Hampton High School.

Mr. Lewis has 39 years of experience in education, 23 of which have been at Hampton High School. He teaches biology, the course in which students are enrolled in during their 10th grade year, a year prior to the academic term in which they take the OEA.

Interview Results

Interviews were conducted with one administrator and five science teachers at Hampton High School in order to find themes related to the low test scores on the Ohio Educational Assessment (OEA) for Science at Hampton High School. First, the researcher made note of the various words or phrases throughout the interview related to the study, identifying specific quotes that support the codes (Creswell, 2015). When each transcript was coded, the codes from each transcript were combined and categorized into themes based on similarity, reducing the codes into a smaller number of categories to be analyzed. Various themes from the qualitative data were identified as reported in Table 1.

Table 1. Codes and Themes from the Interview Data

Themes	Codes	Examples of Participants' Words
Data Analysis	Data	Systems should be in place within the district to mine individual results, aggregate and generalize performance to identify strengths and weaknesses.
	Item analysis	I think it would be interesting to look at the distribution of questions on the OEA and how we're covering those things in curriculum and in what years we're doing it.
	Interpretation	I was confused on how to interpret the assessment data. It would be nice to be able to meet with other professionals on how to interpret this data.
Collaboration	Working together	Grade 11 teachers have been provided with the bank of released questions and scoring guides published by the Ohio DOE, but all teachers use the information independently. It would be beneficial if we could collaborate on this together
	Community	Creating a positive learning community may encourage our students and teachers to work together forming a science club or science fair.
	Team work	There has been discussion about maybe using a team approach to help those lowest achieving students to be pulled up a little bit. This would include the special education teacher and other resources.

	Sharing with others	When teachers share their resources, students benefit.
Professional Development	Teacher learning	There's never been any special effort put into teacher learning regarding the OEAs for Science as far as I'm aware in my tenure in the department.
	In-service	Most teachers seem to want more in-service training session so that they are better trained to support students on the OEA. If teachers were specifically trained on how to support students for the assessment, it is likely that scores could improve.
	Teacher training	Teachers need ongoing support and training in order to help increase scores on the assessment. To my knowledge, there has never been a training session for teachers.
	Certification	It would be nice if teachers could receive some sort of certification before administering the assessment. This may seem far-fetched, but I would imagine that it would help to increase scores.

The researcher identified themes and conducted a word search. The results of the word search can be found in the Frequency Codes Across Interview Data as reported in Table 2.

Table 2. Themes and Frequency Codes Across Interview Data

Themes	Code Word	Occurrences Across Data
Data Analysis	Analysis	9
	Assessments	4

	Data interpretation	7	
Collaboration	Working together	5	
	Community	5	
	Team work	2	
	Sharing with others	3	
Professional Development	Teacher learning	4	
	In-service	3	
	Teacher training	6	
	Certification	7	

Interview Discussion of the Findings

Three overarching themes developed from the interviews. The first was data analysis, the second theme was collaboration, and the third theme was professional development.

Data Analysis. The first theme that was evident was analyzing data. For example, a participant stated, "I was confused on how to interpret the assessment data. It would be nice to be able to meet with other professionals on how to interpret this data." Several participants reported that there is limited time allotted for data analysis among teachers, but that a desire to conduct such analysis exists. Data interpretation seems to be the most difficult aspect of data analysis. Data interpretation was mentioned seven times (see table 2 above) in the interviews as most participants seemed to struggle with understanding the data and applying it to their teaching.

Collaboration. The second theme that was evident was collaboration as numerous teachers expressed an interest in working with fellow teachers. According to one participant, "Grade 11 teachers have been provided with the bank of released questions and scoring guides published by the Ohio DOE, but all teachers use the information independently. It would be beneficial if we could collaborate on this together." Further, teachers desired to work together and felt a sense of community. Both "working together" and "community" were mentioned five times by participants, which reiterated the importance of collaboration. One participant stated, "Creating a positive learning community may encourage our students and teachers to work together forming a science club or science fair." Most participants expressed a desire to share resources with one another and work together to help increase scores on the OEA.

Professional Development. The third theme that was evident was professional development. Professional development was mentioned a total of 20 times in the interviews (see table 2 above). One participant stated that, "There's never been any special effort put into teacher learning regarding the OEAs for Science as far as I'm aware in my tenure in the department." Another teacher said, "Most teachers seem to want more in-service training session so that they are better trained to support students on the OEA. If teachers were specifically trained on how to support students for the assessment, it is likely that scores could improve." Teachers seemed to desire and value ongoing training and an investment in their learning so that they could help the students. Teacher training and certification were also noted as important. One science teacher reiterated that, "Teachers need ongoing support and training in order to help increase scores on the assessment. To my knowledge, there has never been a training session for teachers," which further emphasized the teachers' desire for more professional development. One participant took this one step further and suggested that it would be great if teachers could get, "some sort of certification before administering the assessment."

Survey Findings

The second data collection approach was a survey. The survey contained demographic questions, as well as 15 Likert scale questions. The survey was administered via Survey Monkey. The scale consisted of five possible answers from Strongly Agree to Strongly Disagree and Always to Never.

Survey Description of Participants

Survey participants included 13 teachers at Hampton High School, as well as one special education teacher who worked directly with science, and two administrators, including principals. Of the 16 participants, 3 participants are in the 21 to 29 age range, 4 are in the 30 to 39 range, 4 are in the 40 to 49 range, 2 are in the 50 to 59 range, and 3 are in the 60 or older range. Five administrators participated, along with 2 special education educators, and 9 science teachers. Administrators' average years of service was 10.6 in their current role, while teachers, both special educators and science teachers, had an average tenure of 10.5 years, though it should be noted that two of the participants included in this statistic are in their first year at Hampton High School. Seven of the participants were male, while nine were female. The results of the surveys are reported in Tables 3.

Survey Results

Table 3. Frequency and Average of Survey Responses

Question	Frequency					Avg.
	5	4	3	2	1	
1. Classroom instruction is delivered with the same rigor specified in the NGSS standards.	2	4	6	3	1	3.2
2. Time is provided during contract hours for collaboration between teachers of the *same* courses.	2	2	3	5	4	2.6
3. Data collected from both assessments are used to plan future instruction.	3	4	6	2	1	3.4
4. Content taught in each course is clearly communicated throughout the department.	6	6	2	1	1	3.9
5. Professional development focuses on new instructional strategies has been offered to science teachers.	0	1	3	5	7	1.9

6. Students are excited and ready to learn in my class each day	2	4	5	4	1	3.1
7. Teachers regularly participate in meaningful data analysis conversations.	1	1	1	5	8	1.9
8. The science department at Hampton High School is made of teachers that are highly qualified educators.	3	4	6	3	0	3.4
9. On-going support is provided to new teachers.	3	4	4	3	2	3.2
10. Professional development that serves the instructional needs of teachers is provided on a regular basis.	0	2	3	7	4	2.2

Note: *Averages for each question was calculated by multiplying each response value by the corresponding Likert scale value and summing the results and then dividing the results by the total number of participant responses to the question.*

Survey Discussion of the Findings

Two takeaways emerged. The themes include collaboration and professional development. Based on the survey data, questions 2, 5, 7, and 10 received the lowest ratings. All other questions received above average marks. Question 2 and 7 were of interest, which addressed collaboration. Questions 5 and 10 were of similar interest, which addressed professional development. In the survey, participants indicated that professional development specifically related to instructional strategies has not been offered to science teachers. In fact, question 5 scored an average of 1.9 out of 5—one of the lowest scores of any question on the survey. Because there is a lack of professional development to support instructional practices, it's reasonable to consider that a focus on more frequent professional development on the topic would strengthen instruction within the classroom, which would likely translate to improved scores on the OEA for Science at Hampton High School. Furthermore, meaningful data analysis conversations were another concern among the science faculty at Hampton High School. Participants reported that there is limited time allotted for data analysis conversation among teachers, evidenced by also receiving an average of 1.9 out of 5—another low score on the survey.

Documents Findings

The third data collection approach was documents. Archival data was retrieved from the ODOE website (ODOE, 2019), where test scores from 2015–2016 through 2019–2020 school years are publicly available. The researcher downloaded the data from the website in the form of an Excel file. According to the ODOE, data that is suppressed has been removed from reports in an effort to protect students' privacy (ODOE, 2019). Such suppression was enacted in reporting assessments results for African American, Hispanic, and Asian student groups, as well as for those of two or more races and English language learners.

Documents Results

A review of data was conducted using results from the ODOE regarding the performance of students at Hampton High School on the Ohio Educational Assessment (OEA) for Science. The results of students' performance on the OEA for Science for the three most recent years available are presented in Table 4.

Table 4. Percent of Students Failing to Meet State Expectations on the OEA for Science at Hampton High School

Year	Overall	Male	Female	Socioeconomically Disadvantaged
2015–2016	51.1	48.5	54.1	70.6
2016–2017	40.9	38.7	43.0	46.7
2017–2018	51.9	62.5	36.4	63.9

Mean	48.0	49.9	44.5	60.4

Further analysis was done using a graphical representation of the data. Figure 1 shows percent of students failing to meet state expectations on the OEA for Science at Hampton High School in the form of a trend chart.

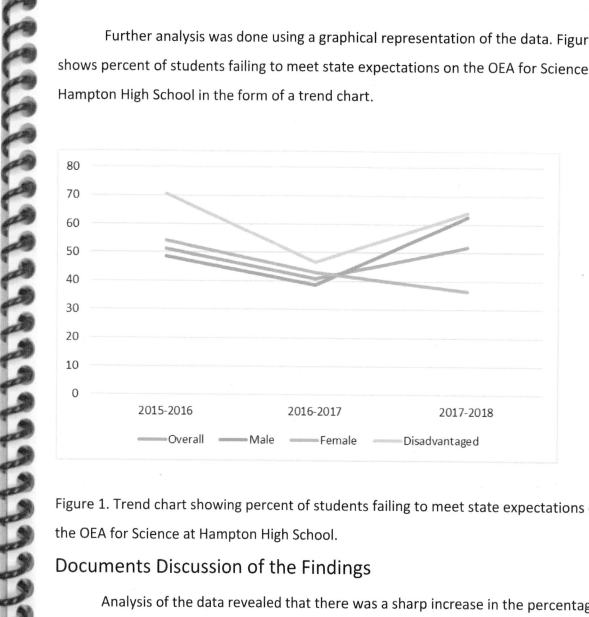

Figure 1. Trend chart showing percent of students failing to meet state expectations on the OEA for Science at Hampton High School.

Documents Discussion of the Findings

Analysis of the data revealed that there was a sharp increase in the percentage of students failing to meet state expectations on the Ohio Educational Assessment (OEA) for Science at Hampton High School particularly for years 2015–2016 and 2017–2018. Of interest was the number of females passing the assessment showed a steady increase while the males showed a decrease in passing the assessment. By 2017 to 2018 the percent of males' failure to meet state expectation on the OEA for science increased to 62.5% whereas the females decreased to 36.4%. Of the socioeconomically disadvantaged students on average, 60.4% failed to meet the expectations set forth by the state, with the highest percentage occurring during the 2015 to 2016 academic year, in which 70.6% of this population did not meet the expectations. However, the failing percentage among these socioeconomically disadvantaged students decreased to 63% over the three-year time frame. The trend chart (See Figure 1) visually displays an increase in all groups except for a decrease among females. A takeaway for this document analysis is that males and socioeconomically disadvantaged students are at the most risk of not meeting the state's expectations for mastery of the science standards and as a result may warrant special attention.

RECOMMENDATIONS

Overview

The purpose of this study was to provide recommendations to the leadership team at Hampton High School with possible solutions to the problem of students' low test scores on the Ohio Educational Assessment (OEA) for Science. In this section, recommendations are presented in an effort to solve the problem of low test scores on the OEA. Additionally, the roles and responsibilities of stakeholders are explained followed by the resources necessary to implement the recommendations and a summary of the recommendations.

Specific Recommendations

The purpose of this study was to provide recommendations to the leadership team at Hampton High School with possible solutions to the problem of students' low test scores on the Ohio Educational Assessment (OEA) for Science. The central research question for this study was, "How can the problem of low test scores on the Ohio Educational Assessment for Science be solved at Hampton High School?" After careful analysis of the data collected in this study, the two most effective solutions recommended to solve the central research question are:

(1) establishing professional learning communities (PLCs) at Hampton High School and

(2) providing targeted professional development to teachers to enhance professional practice.

Recommendation for Professional Learning Communities. Based on the literature, surveys, and interviews, a recommendation to solve this problem of low test scores on the OEA for science is to develop professional learning communities. A professional learning community is a team of teachers who work together to increase student achievement. These communities are deemed effective based on outcomes (DuFour, 2004).

Teachers in an interview expressed a desire to work as a team to increase student achievement. After reviewing the interview transcripts, it was noted that many of the teachers stated that they wanted to work together, especially concerning data analysis. Teachers used words such as "community," "team work," "analysis," and "data interpretation." The usage of these words led the researcher to recommend professional learning communities as one possible solution to the problem of low test scores on the OEA in Science. One participant stated, that by creating a positive learning community, it may inspire teachers and students to work together to form a science club or science fair. This teacher noted that creating either of these without collaboration with other teachers would be impossible, but with other teachers' assistance, students may be motivated to join the science club or science fair, which may lead to students learning more about scientific concepts, and thus may result in increased OES for science scores.

A professional learning community will help solve this problem because a professional learning community would offer teachers the opportunity to "work together" and to create a sense of "community," both of which were codes for this study. One of the most critical steps that educators should take to ensure that students are prepared for high-stakes testing is to ensure that instructional practices are well-aligned to the standards assigned to the course. A common way to accomplish this is by "unpacking" a standard—"the process of taking the text of each standard and translating it into actual teaching strategies" (WiseWire, 2016, para. 1). Establishing a professional learning community should allow teachers the opportunity to work toward aligning the science curriculum with the standards. According to DuFour (2004), professional learning communities require teachers to "focus on learning rather than teaching, work collaboratively on matters related to learning, and hold itself accountable for the kind of results that fuel continual improvement" (p. 8). One goal of the professional learning communities at Hampton High School would be to align the science curriculum to improve student learning opportunities. Teachers expressed a desire to focus on student learning and work collaboratively. The evidence of the effectiveness of a professional development community would be the outcome of future OEA in Science scores.

The professional learning community could improve teacher's data analysis skills. One principal in a study by DuFour (2004) noted that the critical first step in a professional learning community implemented in her school was that the staff began to honestly confront data on student achievement and to work together to improve results rather than make excuses for a lack of improvement. Teachers at Hampton High School expressed a strong desire to use data, but also expressed a lack of fully understanding how to use the data to improve test scores. Professional Learning communities would offer the teachers at Hampton High School the opportunity to collaborate effectively to learn how to analyze and interpret data and to use that information to strategically and collaboratively determine how to help improve students' scores on the OEA in Science.

The implications of implementing professional learning communities at Hampton High School are that students and teachers may benefit from teachers working collaboratively to improve student achievement. For a professional learning community, each team uses student learning evidence to identify specific students who need additional support and time. Further, the team also determines "problematic areas of the curriculum that require the attention of the team, and to help each member become aware of his or her instructional strengths and weaknesses" (DuFour, 2009, p. 1). Utilizing professional learning communities as a method to analyze student data offers teachers an authentic means of decision making. The implementation of professional learning communities has a direct benefit for students in that their learning is closely monitored. The professional learning communities require that formative assessment data be analyzed, and students' performance is enhanced, whether they are falling behind or excelling, through remediation and enrichment opportunities. Thus, all students stand to benefit from the implementation of professional learning communities.

Recommendation for Professional Development. Based on the literature, surveys, and interviews, the second recommendation to solve this problem of low test scores on the OEA for Science is to create professional development opportunities for teachers that are specific to the themes developed in the study. Professional Development is defined as "structured professional learning that results in changes in teacher practices and improvements in student learning outcomes" (Darling-Hammond et al., 2017, p. 1). Research conducted by Ronfeldt et al. (2013) revealed a correlation between a teacher's educational background and professional development acquired and students' performance. Additionally, the same research identified a correlation between teacher collaboration and positive effects on test scores, thus professional development was recommended to improve scores on the OEA for Science.

After reviewing the interview transcripts, it was noted that many of the teachers stated the desire for more professional development. Three participants stated, that by creating professional development, teachers may be able to better understand the data regarding the OEA for science, which may help them to understand the specific deficits of the students' knowledge, which would allow them to design learning opportunities to specifically target science skills where students were deficient. Participants used words such as, "teacher learning," "in-service," "teacher training," and "certification." The repetition of these words led the researcher to determine that professional development could help increase scores on the OEA for Science at Hampton High School. Most participants expressed a desire to share resources with one another and work together to help increase scores on the OEA.

Professional development will help solve this problem of low test scores on the OEA because an in-service on how to analyze data and how to use that data to improve test scores can be developed to specifically address the needs of students at this site. Additionally, males and disadvantaged students were noted on the trend chart as needing their scores improved, thus professional development for teachers for these two populations could be created. According to the National Education Association (n.d.), "Student achievement depends on supporting and educating the whole student. To have high standards for students, there must be high standards for the staff members who work with them" (p. 1). Thus, providing teachers at Hampton High School with quality professional development is likely to lead to more knowledgeable teachers who may then pass this knowledge on to students, who are likely to see an increase in their OEA for Science scores. The evidence of professional development could be the results of the future OEA for science scores.

The implications of implementing professional development for teachers at Hampton High School is that teachers and students may benefit. Students may benefit from potential college and scholarship opportunities based on high scores on the OEA for Science. Teacher skills and knowledge may increase in specific deficit areas of concern such as males and disadvantaged student populations. Targeted instruction and increased efficacy are possible benefits. Clearly, professional development takes time and may be costly, but it is likely that the benefits will outweigh the cons.

Both of these recommendations are designed to enrich student learning and empower teachers to spearhead positive changes as they continue to develop the skills and knowledge related to standards-aligned instruction and data analysis practices through PLCs and professional development opportunities designed to solve the problem of low OEA test scores at Hampton High School.

Roles and Responsibilities of Stakeholders

Professional Learning Communities

In order to solve the problem of students' low test scores on the Ohio Educational Assessment (OEA) for Science, it is recommended that professional learning communities be implemented at Hampton High School. Defining the roles and responsibilities of those involved in the professional learning communities is important to ensure success.

Administrators. The role of administrators in professional learning communities would be to determine the purpose and goals, along with the teachers' input. Administration would monitor the overall process and progress of the professional learning communities as a means of ensuring effectiveness. Implementing any new initiative may be met with some skepticism, especially in the case of Hampton High School where interview participants indicated that a flurry of district-based initiatives have come and gone in recent years, many without reaching fruition. As such, teachers may be reluctant to begin the on-boarding process to a new strategy for improving students' success. However, Jessie (2012) recommended the following:

1. Allow staff to see success with the process from other schools with similar demographics.
2. Share a personal vision that is genuine and contagious regarding the benefit of PLCs.
3. Find the connection between short-term goals and progress and the school's mission statement and vision.
4. Allow teachers that share the same vision to take owner- and authorship of the work done in PLCs.

Thus, administrators would act as a facilitator of the personal learning communities by offering guidance and support, and who would serve as an accountability partner. Administrations would not need to hire new staff to implement or support the personal learning communities, as administrators and teachers would be responsible for all aspects required.

Teachers. The role of teachers in creating and implementing professional learning communities would be to help create the goals and purpose, along with administration, and then to carry out and participate in the professional learning communities. The primary function of professional learning communities is to provide a uniform approach to planning and evaluating curriculum and learning through the use of a cyclic process that can be carried from one topic to another throughout the school year; thus, teachers should work together to ensure that science topics are appropriately scaffolded from one grade-level to the next. Collaboration, which was one of the themes that developed in the interviews and surveys, is a critical component of the success of professional learning communities.

To learn how to implement professional learning communities, professional development from an outside source, such as that of Solution Tree, the organization founded by Richard DuFour, the developer of professional learning communities, is recommended. This professional development will allow administrators and teachers to gain an understanding of the process and purpose of professional learning communities, including the three main ideas, which are to: focus on student learning, focus on collaboration, and focus on results—and learn how to customize it to meet the specific needs at Hampton High School (Solution Tree, 2020b, para. 4).

Professional Development

In order to solve the problem of students' low test scores on the Ohio Educational Assessment (OEA) for Science, it is recommended that professional development be implemented at Hampton High School. Roles and responsibilities of those involved in the professional development are important to define to ensure success.

Administrators. The role of administrators in regard to professional development would be to oversee and facilitate the process while the curriculum specialist would be in charge of the content of the professional development based on the results of this research. Multiple sessions of professional development are recommended to address the themes of this research including data analysis, collaboration, and professional development. Professional development should be an on-going and job-embedded experience. Job-embedded learning "means that professional development is a continuous thread that can be found throughout the culture of the school" (Education World, 2012, para. 2).

Teachers. Professional development sessions should include all faculty and support staff who would be required to attend all three professional development sessions, thus one role of the teacher is to attend all professional development sessions. The first professional development session should include information regarding the scaffolding and differentiation of instruction in a way that builds students' understandings to a mastery level, aligning itself with the goals of the professional learning communities. The second professional development should include how to work collaboratively, using data, to improve student achievement, again, this information would become part of the goals of the personal learning communities. The third professional development session would address how teachers can work together to target specific groups of students who have historically scored low on the OEA for Science including males and disadvantaged students. The primary function of the three professional development sessions is to build teachers' familiarity and efficacy with data analysis, collaboration, and professional development opportunities to increase scores on the OEA for Science for students at Hampton High School.

Resources Needed

Professional Learning Communities

It is advisable that teachers have similar schedules beyond that of planning to facilitate shared remediation and enrichment opportunities for students. Ideally, at least two teachers would be teaching the same course, though perhaps at different levels, during the same period. When such a schedule is in place, teachers are able to switch students between classrooms for targeted, homogenous groupings to help students make greater academic gains. In situations where only two teachers are assigned to a course, such as those at the 11th and 12th grade levels, this task may become more challenging, which, again, leads to the suggestion a revision of the course offerings schedule (and thus teachers schedules) to allow for more effective teacher collaboration and to better meet the needs of males and disadvantaged students, and those students who may be struggling with a particular topic. This recommendation requires time to make changes, but there is no financial cost other than time to redistribute course offerings.

Solution Tree (2020a), the company started by Richard DuFour, the pioneer of professional learning communities, offers a variety of 2-day trainings that focus on different aspects of professional learning communities. To attend one of these workshops costs US$689 per person. For the entire science department at Hampton High School, plus the special educator that works most exclusively with the science department, as well as the four school administrators who would provide on-going support for the department, the total cost would be US$10,335, plus the cost of travel and accommodations for each participant. This cost includes the two-day workshop along with opportunities to work within collaborative teams to begin the early work of establishing a professional learning community. Participants will leave the seminar with access to a variety of tools to help ensure the success of their communities as the return to Hampton High School.

Because this cost is extensive, it is reasonable to consider sending only key individuals to the two-day session with the charge of bringing information back to the rest of the department and administrators. If this were to be the case, the cost could be reduced to as little as US$3,445, plus travel and accommodations. Access to the same materials would be provided for use within the groups, but additional time would be needed to work through the primary steps of establishing professional learning communities among content-related teachers, as only a limited number of teachers would be attending the training.

Professional Development

Aside from the aforementioned professional development needed to implement professional learning communities effectively, time is also needed to host professional development for teachers and administrators related to data analysis, collaboration, and professional development. This includes time in August prior to the school year starting, as well as on-going professional development throughout the school year. Because time is a limited resource, especially once the school year begins, some of this on-going learning can take place during the late start days or during professional learning communities time, as the benefit of this professional development is directly applicable to both the professional learning communities and student learning. It should be viewed, however, as an extension to the professional learning communities work rather than a replacement for typical professional learning communities work.

Professional development is time costly, but it can be rather inexpensive or even free. Other than the professional development for the professional learning communities, the three recommended professional development sessions can be developed at no cost by utilizing resources that are readily available such as information on the internet and the possible creation of three PowerPoint presentations. Teachers may work collaboratively in their processional learning communities to create professional development or administrators may allow teachers to take professional development online from professionals such as a website called Model Teaching. Model Teaching (Model Teaching, 2020) offers a course called *Intro to Documentation and Data Analysis* for about US$20 per teacher. The cost for the entire science department would be approximately US$140. If administrators were included in the professional development, the cost would be approximately US$200. If teachers and administrators participated in three sessions of professional development each, the total cost of the professional development would be approximately US$600. If significant changes are to be made regarding students' learning and their performance on assessments such as the OEA for Science, professional learning communities and professional development are an investment in the students' academic achievement opportunities.

Timeline

Professional Learning Communities

Implementation of the professional learning communities will take approximately eight months. See Table 5 for Timeline of Professional Learning Communities Implementation.

Table 5. Timeline of Professional Learning Communities Implementation

Date	Action Item
January 1, 2021	Introduce the concept of professional learning communities.
February 2, 2021	Science teachers visit another school that currently practices professional learning communities.
February 3, 2021	Teachers share experiences from yesterday's visit.
February 10, 2021	Faculty meeting to discuss the connection between the purpose (including goals and objectives) of the professional learning communities and the mission and vision of the school.

March 1, 2021	Faculty meeting to determine the goals and objectives of the professional learning communities.
March 7, 2021	Continued planning for the professional learning communities. Monthly and yearly goals and objectives should be established in writing.
March 14, 2021	Continued planning for the professional learning communities. More specific detail regarding the monthly and yearly goals and objectives should be written.
April 4, 2021	Determine a timeline for implementation of professional learning communities beginning in the fall of the new school year.
August 19, 2021	One week prior to the first day of school, administrators and staff will revisit the goals and objectives of the professional learning communities.
August 20, 2021	First professional learning communities meeting.
August, 2021+	Implement professional learning communities. Goals and objectives should be monitored throughout the year.

Professional Development

Implementation of the professional development will take approximately five months. See Table 6 for Timeline of Professional Development Implementation.

Table 6. Timeline of Professional Learning Communities Implementation

Date	Action Item
January 14, 2021	Administration decides on professional development options
January 16, 2021	Administration works with teachers to decide on the three most needed topics of professional development based on the data
February 22, 2021	Administration and teachers work together to secure or

	create professional development based on the last meeting (purchase online or create)
February 2, 2021	Announce first professional development at faculty meeting
March 15, 2021	First professional development
March 15, 2021	Announce second professional development at faculty meeting
April 15, 2021	Second professional development
April 15, 2021	Announce third professional development at faculty meeting
May 15, 2021	Third professional development

Summary

The goal of this study was to identify factors that impact students' performance on the Ohio Educational Assessment for Science at Hampton High School, a suburban high school located in southeastern Ohio. Identifying factors that impacted OEA scores was important since the OEA for Science is one of the publicly available indicators of students' learning. By utilizing data from interviews, an online survey, and a review of documents, it became evident that improvements could be made to help improve students' scores on the OEA for science. This research established the importance of creating professional learning communities and professional development to help increase student's scores on the OEA for Science at Hampton High School.

REFERENCES

American University. (2018, May 4). *What makes professional development effective for teachers?* https://soeonline.american.edu/blog/what-makes-professional-development-for-teachers-effective

Aucejo, E. M., & Romano, T. F. (2016). Assessing the effect of school days and absences on test score performance. *Economics of Education Review, 55*(1), 70–87. https://doi.org/10.1016/j.econedurev.2016.08.007

Battelle for Kids. (2011). *Successfully implementing transformational change in education: Lessons learned about the importance of effective change leadership and strategic communications.* https://www2.ed.gov/programs/racetothetop/communities/bfk-rttt-communications-lessons-learned.pdf

Bertolini, K., Stremmel, A., & Thorngren, J. (2012). *Student achievement factors* (ED569687). ERIC. https://files.eric.ed.gov/fulltext/ED568687.pdf

Bickman, L., & Rog, D. J. (2009). *The SAGE handbook of applied social research methods* (2nd ed.). SAGE.

Blatchford, P., Chan, K. W., Galton, M., Lai, K. C., & Lee, J. C. (Eds.). (2016). *Class size: Eastern and Western perspectives*. Routledge.

Boynton, M., & Boynton, C. (2005). *The educator's guide to preventing and solving discipline problems*. ASCD.

California County Superintendents Educational Services Association. (2016, June). *Best practices in teacher and administrator induction programs*. http://ccsesa.org/wp-content/uploads/2016/06/Best-Practices-in-Teacher-and-Administrator-Induction-Programs.pdf

Carnegie Mellon University. (n.d.). *Why should assessments, learning objectives, and instructional strategies be aligned?* https://www.cmu.edu/teaching/assessment/basics/alignment.html

Case, B., & Zucker, S. (2005). *Horizontal and vertical alignment* [Policy Report]. Pearson.
https://images.pearsonassessments.com/images/tmrs/tmrs_rg/HorizontalVertic
alAlignment.pdf?WT.mc_id=TMRS_Horizontal_and_Vertical_Alignment

Cerezo, L. (n.d.). *Standardized testing*. Universidad de Murcia.
https://webs.um.es/lourdesc/miwiki/lib/exe/fetch.php?id=units&cache=cache&
media=standardized_testing.pdf

Chingos, M. M. (2010). *The impact of universal class-zie reduction policy: Evidence from
Florida's statewide mandate*. Harvard University.

Christensen, V. (2018). What makes a test standardized? *The Classroom*. Retrieved
from https://www.theclassroom.com/test-standardized-6680561.html

Clay, V. (2016, May 11). *Intrinsic motivation vs. standardized tests*. Edutopia.
https://www.edutopia.org/blog/intrinsic-motivation-vs-standardized-tests-
valencia-clay

Cole, R. W. (2008). Educating everybody's children: Diverse teaching strategies for
diverse learners
http://www.ascd.org/publications/books/107003/chapters/Educating-
Everybody%27s-Children@-We-Know-What-Works%E2%80%94And-What-
Doesn%27t.aspx

College Board. (2019a). *Test dates and deadlines*.
https://collegereadiness.collegeboard.org/sat/register/dates-deadlines

College Board. (2019b). *SAT school day Apr 09, 2019, 11th grade—question analysis—
Form R Evidenced-based reading and writing questions*.
https://collegereadiness.collegeboard.org/sat/register/dates-deadlines

Creswell, J. W. (2015). *Educational research: Planning, conducting, and evaluating
quantitative and qualitative research*. Pearson Education.

Creswell, J. W., & Poth, C. N. (2019). *Qualitative inquiry & research design: Choosing
among five approaches*. SAGE.

Curry, D. P., Reeves, E., McIntyre, C. J., & Capps, M. (2018). Do teacher credentials matter? An examination of teacher quality. *Curriculum and Teaching Dialogue, 20*(1/2), 9–180.

Cuseo, J. (2007). The empirical case against large class size: Adverse effects on the teaching, learning, and retention of first-year students. *Journal of Faculty Development, 21*(5), 5–21.

Darling-Hammond, L. (2015). Can value added add value to teacher evaluation? *Educational Researcher, 44*(2), 132–137.

Darling-Hammond, L., Hyler, M. E., & Gardner, M. (2017, June 5). *Effective teacher professional development.* https://learningpolicyinstitute.org/product/effective-teacher-professional-development-report

Darling-Hammond, L., & Youngs, P. (2002). Defining highly qualified teachers: What does scientifically based research actually tell us? *Educational Researcher, 31*(9), 13–25.

Davies, R. (2019). 5 reasons your students misbehave for a substitute & how to prevent it. *Differentiated TEACHING.* Retrieved from https://www.thethirdwheelteacher.com/why-students-misbehave-for-the-substitute/

Davies, R. (2019). *5 reasons your students misbehave for a substitute & how to prevent it.* Differentiated TEACHING. https://www.thethirdwheelteacher.com/why-students-misbehave-for-the-substitute/

DeMonte, J. (2015). *A million new teachers are coming: Will they be ready to teach?* American Institutes for Research. https://www.air.org/sites/default/files/downloads/report/Million-New-Teachers-Brief-deMonte-May-2015.pdf

Donaldson, G. A. (2014). *From schoolhouse to schooling system: Ohio public education in the 20th century.* College of Education and Human Development, University of Ohio.

Drake, S. M., & Burns, R. G. (2004). *Meeting standards through integrated curriculum.* ASCD.

DuFour, R. (2004). What is a professional learning community? *Educational Leadership, 61*(8), 6–11.

DuFour, R. (2004). What is a professional learning community? *Educational Leadership, 61*(8), 6–11.

DuFour, R. (2009). *Professional learning communities: The key to improving teaching and learning.* Cognia. https://www.advanc-ed.org/source/professional-learning-communities-key-improved-teaching-and-learning

Dweck, C. (2000). *Self-theories: Their role in motivation, personality and development.* Taylor & Francis.

Education World. (2012). *How to facilitate job-embedded professional development.* https://www.educationworld.com/a_admin/job-embedded-professional-development.shtml

Education World. (2019). *Boosting test scores: Principal strategies that work.* https://www.educationworld.com/a_admin/admin/admin366.shtml

EF Academy. (2019). *10 benefits of small class sizes* [Blog]. https://www.ef.com/wwen/blog/efacademyblog/10-benefits-small-class-sizes/

https://www.ef.com/wwen/blog/efacademyblog/10-benefits-small-class-sizes/

Ehrenberg, R. G., & Brewer, D. J. (1995). Did teachers' verbal ability and race matter in the 1960s? Coleman revisited. *Economics of Education Review, 14*(1), 1–21. https://doi.org/10.1016/0272-7757(94)00031-Z

Ellis, S. (2018, April 23). Why standardizes tests matter beyond college admissions. *U.S. News & World Report.* https://www.usnews.com/education/blogs/college-admissions-playbook/articles/2018-04-23/3-benefits-of-standardized-testing-beyond-college-admissions

Finn, J. D., Pannozzo, G. M., & Achilles, C. M. (2003). The why's of class size: Student behavior in small classes. *Review of Educational Research, 73*(3), 321–368.

Fischer, C., Fishman, B., Dede, C., Eisenkraft, A., Frumin, K., Foster, B., & McCoy, A. (2018). Investigating relationships between school context, teacher professional development, teaching practices, and student achievement in response to a nationwide reform. *Teaching and Teacher Education*, *72*(1), 107–121. https://doi.org/10.1016/j.tate.2018.02.011

Frey, B. B. (Ed). (2018). *The SAGE encyclopedia of educational research, measurement, and evaluation.* https://doi.org/10.4135/9781506326139.n340

Gallagher, C. J. (2003). Reconciling a tradition of testing with a new paradigm. *Educational Psychology Review*, *15*(1), 83–99. https://doi.org/10.1023/A:1021323509290

Gallagher, N. K. (2015). *New assessment tests for Ohio students.* Portland Press Herald: Schools and Education. https://www.pressherald.com/new-tests-for_ohio-pupils-to-be-rolled-out/

Garcia, L. E., & Thornton, O. (2014, November 18). The enduring importance of parental involvement. *NEA Today.* http://neatoday.org/2014/11/18/the-enduring-importance-of-parental-involvement-2/

Glossary of Education Reform. (2015). *Norm-referenced test.* The Glossary of Education Reform. https://www.edglossary.org/norm-referenced-test/

Greenberg, M. (2014). It's time for a new definition of accreditation. *The Chronicle of Higher Education*, *60*(20).

Greenville Public School District. (n.d.). *New teacher induction program.* https://www.gvillepublicschooldistrict.com/docs/district/depts/20/greenville%20public%20school%20district%20new%20teacher%20induction%20program.pdf?id=3990

Hampton High School. (2019). *Hampton High School program of studies 2019–2020.* https://www.hamptonhighschooleagles.org

Hawker Brownlow Education. (n.d.). *Quick reference guide: Criterion-referenced vs. norm-referenced assessment.*

http://files.hbe.com.au/flyerlibrary/Brigance/Criterion-referenced%20vs.%20Norm-referenced%20Assessment.pdf

Heck, R. H., & Hallinger, P. (2014). Modeling the longitudinal effects of school leadership on teaching and learning. *Journal of Educational Administration, 52*(5), 653–681.

Herman, J. L., Osmundson, E., & Dietel, R. (2010). *Benchmark assessment for improved learning* (AACC Report). University of California.

Higgins, J. (2014, October 28). *Does class size matter? Research reveals surprises.* The Seattle Times. https://www.seattletimes.com

Hoxby, C. M. (1998). *The effect of class size on student achievements: New evidence from population variation.* NBER Working Papers 6869, National Bureau of Economic Research, Inc.

Hulleman, C. S., & Hulleman, T. (2018). *An important piece of the student motivation puzzle.* https://www.future-ed.org/reversing-the-decline-in-student-motivation/

Ingersoll, R. M. (2012, May 16). *Beginning teacher induction: What the data tell us.* Education Week. https://www.edweek.org/ew/articles/2012/05/16/kappan_ingersoll.h31.html

Ingersoll, R. M., & Strong, M. (2011). The impact of induction and mentoring programs for beginning teachers: A review of the research. *Review of Educational Research, 81*(2), 201–233.

Jacobson, L. (2018, March 28). *Standards for teacher induction programs released.* New Teacher Center. https://newteachercenter.org/news-story/standards-for-teacher-induction-programs-released/

Jessie, L. G. (2012, January 4). *Creating buy-in for PLCs.* All Things PLC. https://www.allthingsplc.info/blog/view/161/creating-buy-in-for-plcs

Johnson, E., & Semmelroth, C. L. (2014). Special education teacher evaluation: Why it matters, what makes it challenging, and how to address these challenges. *Assessment for Effective Intervention, 39*(2), 71–82.

Kalenze, E. (2016, December 26). *How positive student–teacher relationships impact student motivation* [Blog]. Search Institute. https://www.search-institute.org/positive-teacher-student-relationships-impact-student-motivation/

Kielwitz, H. A. (2014). *Comprehensive teacher induction: Linking teacher induction to theory* (ED557137). ERIC. https://files.eric.ed.gov/fulltext/ED557137.pdf

Klein, A. (2018). *How does science testing work under ESSA? Politics K-12: Your Education Roadmap*. Education Week. http://edweek.org/edweek/campaign-k-12/2018/10/science-essa-testing-states-plans.html

Koedel, C., & Polikoff, M. (2017). Big bang for just a few bucks: The impact of math textbooks in California. *Evidence Speaks Reports, 2*(5), 1–7.

Kosanovich, M., & Rodriguez, E. (2019). *Developing effective teachers through targeted professional development*. Middle School Matters. https://greatmiddleschools.org/developing-effective-teachers-through-targeted-professional-development/

Lavrakas, P. J. (2008). Test–retest reliability. In P. J. Lavrakas (Ed.), *Encyclopedia of Survey Research Methods*. SAGE. https://doi.org/10.4135/9781412963947.n581

Lestrund, M. (2013). Educational interventions. In F. R. Volkmar (Ed.), *Encyclopedia of Autism Spectrum Disorders*. Springer.

Loeb, S., & Figlio, D. (2011). School accountability. In E. A. Hanushek, S. Machin, & L. Woessmann (Eds.), *Handbook of the Economics of Education* (Vol. 3). Elsevier.

Lynch, M. (2016a, August 23). *The pros and con' of alternate-route teacher preparation programs*. The Edvocate. https://www.theedadvocate.org/pros-cons-alternate-route-teacher-preparation-programs/

Lynch, M. (2016b, September 18). *Understanding federal funding part I: 3 types of school funding.* The Edvocate. https://www.theedadvocate.org/understanding-federal-funding-part-3-types-school-funding/

Martinez, L. (2018). *Motivating students before and after testing*. https://engage2learn.org/motivating-students-before-and-after-testing/

Mathewson, T. G. (2019). *How to unlock students' internal drive for learning: Intrinsic motivators can be key to student achievement—but extrinsic motivation dominates classrooms*. The Hechinger Report. https://hechingerreport.org/intrinsic-motivation-is-key-to-student-achievement-but-schools-kill-it/

Matthews, J. (2012, February 25). *Why textbooks don't work and hurt schools*. The Washington Post. https://www.washingtonpost.com/blogs/class-struggle/post/why-our-textbooks-dont-work/2012/02/25/gIQAvI16ZR_blog.html?noredirect=on

McKay, S. (2015, September 25). *Using new research to improve student motivation* [Blog]. Carnegie Foundation. https://www.carnegiefoundation.org/blog/using-new-research-to-improve-student-motivation/

Miller, R. T., Murnane, R. J., & Willett, J. B. (2007, August). *Do teacher absences impact student test scores? Longitudinal evidence from one urban school district*. National Bureau of Economic Research. http://www.nber.org/papers/w13356

Model Teaching. (2020). *Intro to documentation and data analysis*. https://www.modelteaching.com

National Association of Elementary School Principles. (n.d.). *Using student achievement data to support instructional decision making*. http://www.naesp.org/sites/default/files/Student_Data_0.pdf

National Center on Response to Intervention. (n.d.). *Using fidelity to enhance program implementation with an RTI framework*. https://rti4success.org/sites/default/files/Using%20Fidelity%20to%20Enhance%20Program%20Implementation_PPTSlides.pdf

National Council of Teachers of English. (2014a). *Why class size matters today* (Position statements). https://ncte.org/statement/why-class-size-matters/

National Council of Teachers of English. (2014b). *How standardized tests shape and limit student learning*.

https://secure.ncte.org/library/NCTEFiles/Resources/Journals/CC/0242-
nov2014/CC0242PolicyStandardized.pdf

National Education Association. (2019a). *History of standardized testing in the United States*. http://www.nea.org/home/66139.htm

National Education Association. (2019b). *Status of substitute teachers: A state-by-state summary*. http://www.nea.org/home/14813.htm

National Education Association. (n.d.). *Professional development*. http://www.nea.org/home/30998.htm

Nest, P. (2019). *Test prep & review strategies for grades 6–8*. National Education Association. http://www.nea.org/tools/lessons/Test-Prep-Review-Strategies-Grades-6-8.htm

New Teacher Center. (2016a). *Analysis of student work: Providing mentors with tools and strategies to help beginning teachers identify student needs, plan for differentiated instruction, and ensure equitable learning outcomes*. https://newteachercenter.org

New Teacher Center. (2016b). *Coaching and observation strategies: Guiding mentors in the collection and analysis of classroom observations*. https://newteachercenter.org

New Teacher Center. (2016c). *Mentor formative assessment and support: Promoting growth*. https://newteachercenter.org

New Teacher Center. (2019). *Our approach*. https://newteachercenter.org/our-approach

No Child Left Behind Act of 2001, P.L. 107-110, 20 U.S.C. § 6319 (2002).

Ohio Department of Education. (1990). *Ohio's common core of learning*. Ohio Department of Educational and Cultural Services.

Ohio Department of Education. (2018a). *2017–18 OEA science test designs*. https://www.Ohio.gov/doe/sites/ohio.gov.doe/files/inline-files/2017-18TestDesignSheet.pdf

Ohio Department of Education. (2018b). *Achievement level descriptors and score ranges.*

>https://www.Ohio.gov/doe/sites/ohio.gov.doe/files/inline-

>files/MEA_2018_ALDs%2BCut%20Scores_10-09-18.pdf

Ohio Department of Education. (2018c). O*hio comprehensive assessment system*

>*(MECAS).* https://www.Ohio.gov/doe/Testing_Accountability/MECAS

Ohio Department of Education. (2018d). *OEA science.*

>https://www.ohio.gov/doe/Testing_Accountability/MECAS/material/meascience

Ohio Department of Education. (2019). *Ohio student performance on state assessments.*

>https://public.tableau.com/profile/ohio.department.of.education/Assessments

Ohio Department of Education. (2020a). Ohio assessment and accountability reporting

>system (MAARS). https://lms.backpack.education/public/Ohio

Ohio Department of Education. (2020b). *The Ohio educational assessments: Why*

>*participation matters.* Ohio Department of Education.

>https://www.ohio.gov/doe/sites/.gov.doe/files/inline-

>files/Why%20Participation%20Matters-1.pdf

Ohio School Administrative District 75. (2019). *State assessment FAQs.*

>http://link.org/district/teaching_and_learning/state_assessment_a_qs

Okeke, C. I. O., Shumba, J., Rembe, S., & Sotuku, N. (2015). Demographic variables,

>work stimulated stressors and coping strategies of pre-school educators: A

>concept paper. *Journal of Psychology, 6*(1), 91–101.

O'Malley, K. (2012). *Standardized testing: What is it and how does it work?* Pearson.

>https://www.pearsoned.com/standardized-testing-work/

Osborne, M. (2018). *The class size debate: 5 important findings from research.* North

>Carolina Center for Public Policy Research. https://nccppr.org/class-size-debate-

>5-important-findings-research/

Phelan, C., & Wren, J. (2006). *Exploring reliability in academic assessment.*

>https://chfasoa.uni.edu/reliabilityandvalidity.htm

Pianta, R. C., & Ansari, A. (2018). Does attendance in private schools predict student outcomes at age 15? Evidence from a longitudinal study. *Educational Researcher, 47*(7), 419–434. https://doi.org/10.3102/0013189X18785632

Piro, J. S., Dunlap, K., & Shutt, T. (2014). A collaborative data chat: Teaching summative assessment data use in pre-service teacher education. *Cogent Education, 1*(1), 968409.

Renaissance (2018). *What is the difference between criterion-referenced and norm-referenced testing?* https://www.renaissance.com/2018/07/11/blog-criterion-referenced-tests-norm-referenced-tests/

Ronfeldt, M., Loeb, S., & Wyckoff, J. (2013). How teacher turnover harms student achievement. *American Educational Research Journal, 50*(1), 4-36. doi:10.3102/0002831212463813

Salkind, N. J. (2010). Parallel forms reliability. In N. J. Salkind (Ed.), *Encyclopedia of Research Design*. SAGE. https://doi.org/10.4135/9781412961288.n301

Sierra, R. (2015). *What is reflective teaching and why is it important?* RichmondShare. https://www.richmondshare.com.br/what-is-reflective-teaching-and-why-is-it-important/

Solomon, S. (2016). *What makes an effective teacher induction program?* Go Public Schools Oakland. https://gopublicschoolsoakland.org/2016/12/what-makes-an-effective-teacher-induction-program/

Solution Tree. (2020a). *2-day workshops.* https://www.solutiontree.com/events/workshops.html

Solution Tree. (2020b). *Our on-site professional learning for PLC at Work.* https://www.solutiontree.com/plc-at-work/pd-services

Springer, M. G. (2008). *Accountability incentives: Do school practice educational triage?* EducationNext. https://www.educationnext.org/accountability-incentives/

Stansbury, K., & Zimmerman, J. (2000). *Lifelines to the classroom: Designing support for beginning teachers.* WestEd. https://www.wested.org/online_pubs/tchrbrief.pdf

Stassen, M., Doherty, K., & Poe, M (2001). Program-based review and assessment: Tools and techniques for program improvement. Office of Academic Planning and Assessment, University of Massachusetts, Amherst. https://www.umass.edu/oapa/tools-and-services/assessment-handbooks

Steelman, S. (2018). How to mentor new teachers so they won't quit. *School Leaders Now*. https://schoolleadersnow.weareteachers.com/mentor-new-teachers/

Stenger, M. (2014). *5 research-based tips for providing students with meaningful feedback*. Edutopia. https://www.edutopia.org/blog/tips-providing-students meaningful-feedback-marianne-stenger

Stone, M. (2018). How Ohio hurt education by trying to reform it. *Daily News: Focus*. https://dailynews.com/2017/11/14/focus/how-hurt-education-by-trying-to-reform-it/

Stronge, J. H. (2018). *Qualities of effective teachers* (3rd ed.). ASCD.

Teaching Tolerance. (2019). *Teaching teachers: PD to improve student achievement*. https://www.tolerance.org/professional-development/teaching-teachers-pd-to-improve-student-achievement

Thijs, J., & Fleischmann, F. (2015). Student-teacher relationships and achievement goal orientations: Examining student perceptions in an ethnically diverse sample. *Elsevier, 42*, 52-63. https://doi.org/10.1016/j.lindif.2015.08.014

Thompson, J. (1998). *Discipline survival kit for the secondary teacher*. The Centre for Applied Research in Education.

Tyner, A. (2018). *When students take tests, are they actually trying?* Thomas B. Fordham Institute. https://fordhaminstitute.org/national/commentary/when-students-take-tests-are-they-actually-trying

University of Missouri-Columbia. (2018). *Students taught by highly qualified teachers more likely to obtain bachelor's degree: Schools with more teachers who majored in their teaching subject are more likely to have students succeed both short and long term*. Science Daily. https://www.sciencedaily.com/releases/2018/05/180522114820.htm

Urbandale Community School District. (2019). 627—*Instructional materials: Selection, inspection, and reconsideration.* http://www.urbandaleschools.com/policy/article-600-educational-program/627-instructional-materials-selection-inspection-and-reconsideration/

U.S. Congress, Office of Technology Assessment. (1992). *Testing in American schools: Asking the right questions.* U.S. Government Printing Office.

U.S. Department of Education. (2004). New No Child Left Behind flexibility: Highly qualified teachers. https://www2.ed.gov/nclb/methods/teachers/hqtflexibility.html

U.S. Department of Education. (2016). *Overview of proposed regulations: Assessments.* https://www2.ed.gov/policy/elsec/leg/essa/nprmassessmentppt07192016.pdf

U.S. Department of Education Office of Innovation and Improvement. (2004). *Alternative routes to teacher licensure.* Author.

Ware, F. (2002). Black teachers' perceptions of their professional roles. In J. J. Irvine (Ed.), *In search of wholeness: African-American teachers and their culturally specific classroom practices.* Palgrave. 33-45.

Westrick, P. A., Le, H., Robbins, S. B., Radunzel, J. M., & Schmidt, F. L. (2015). College performance and retention: A meta-analysis of the predictive validities of ACT® scores, high school grades, and SES. *Educational Assessment, 20*(1), 23–45.

Whelan, D. L. (2008). Teacher absenteeism affects student achievement. *School Library Journal, 1*(10), 1–10.

Wiggins, G. P., & McTighe, J. (2005). *Understanding by design* (2nd ed.). ASCD.

Wilcox, D. R., & Samaras, A. P. (2009). Examining our career switching teachers' first year of teaching: Implications for alternative teacher education program design. *Teacher Education Quarterly, 36*(4), 173–191.

William, D. (2018). *Embedded formative assessment* (2nd ed.). Solution Tree Press.

WiseWire. (2016). *What does it mean to "unpack" a standard?* https://www.wisewire.com/wp-content/uploads/items/54051/pdf_cta_LMD_0022.pdf

Wolf, L. F., & Smith, J. K. (1995). The consequence of consequence: Motivation, anxiety, and test performance. *Applied Measurement in Education*, 8(3), 227–242.

APPENDIX A

August 16, 2019

Hampton High School

101 Rock Point Road

Columbus, Ohio

Dear Suzanna Brawn,

After careful review of your research proposal entitled, *Improving Students' Scores on the Ohio Educational Assessment for Science*, I have decided to grant you permission to conduct your research at Hampton High School in the Columbus, OH.

Sincerely,

Jenny Keller

Jenny J. Keller, Principal

(867) 555-5309

References

Ainley, M., & Ainley, J. (2011). Student engagement with science in early adolescence: The contribution of enjoyment to students' continuing interest in learning about science. *Contemporary Educational Psychology, 36*(1), 4–12. https://doi.org/10.1016/j.cedpsych.2010.08.001

Alreck, P. L., & Settle, R. B. (1995). *The survey research handbook: Guidelines and strategies for conducting a survey.* Irwin Professional.

American Psychological Association. (2019). *Peer review.* https://www.apa.org/pubs/journals/resources/peer-review

Bandura, A. (1997). *Self-efficacy: The exercise of control.* Worth.

Bickman, L., & Rog, D. J. (Eds.). (2009). *The SAGE handbook of applied social research methods* (2nd ed.). SAGE.

Creswell, J. W. (2015). *A concise introduction to mixed methods research.* SAGE.

Creswell, J. W., & Poth, C. N. (2018). *Qualitative inquiry & research design: Choosing among five approaches* (4th ed.). SAGE.

Eagly, A. H., & Chaiken, S. (2007). The advantages of an inclusive definition of attitude. *Social Cognition, 25*(5), 582–602. https://doi.org/10.1521/soco.2007.25.5.582

Gall, M. D., Borg, W. R., & Gall, J. P. (1996). *Educational research: An introduction* (6th ed.). Longman.

Gall, M. D., Gall, J. P., & Borg, W. R. (2006). *Educational research: An introduction* (8th ed.). Allyn & Bacon.

Gobbo, K., & Shmulsky, S. (2014). Faculty experiences with college students with autism spectrum disorders: A qualitative study of challenges and solutions. *Focus on Autism and Other Developmental Disabilities, 29*(1), 13–22. https://doi.org/10.1177/1088357613504989

Greenberg, M. (2014). It's time for a new definition of accreditation. *The Chronicle of Higher Education, 60*(20).

Lynch, M. (2016a). The pro's and con's of alternate-route teacher preparation programs. https://www.theedadvocate.org/pros-cons-alternate-route-teacher-preparation-programs/

Lynch, M. (2016b). Understanding federal funding part I: 3 types of school funding. *The Edvocate.* https://www.theedadvocate.org/understanding-federal-funding-part-3-types-school-funding/

Maslow, A. H. (1943). A theory of human motivation. *Psychological Review, 50*(4), 370–396. https://doi.org/10.1037/h0054346

Maxwell, J. A. (2005). *Qualitative research design: An interactive approach* (2nd ed.). SAGE.

McGuinn, P. (2016). From No Child Left Behind act to the Every Student Succeeds Act: Federalism and the education legacy of the Obama administration. *Publius: The Journal of Federalism, 46*(3), 392–415. https://doi.org/10.1093/publius/pjw014

McLeod, S. (2015). Psychology research ethics. *Simply psychology.* http://www.simplypsychology.org/Ethics.html

Mitchell, W., & Beresford, B. (2014). Young people with high-functioning autism and Asperger's syndrome planning for and anticipating the move to college: What supports a positive transition? *British Journal of Special Education, 41*(2), 151–171. https://doi.org/10.1111/1467-8578.12064

Ohio Department of Education. (n.d.). https//.k.12.assessments.gov

Patton, M. Q. (2002). *Qualitative research & evaluation methods* (3rd ed.) SAGE.

Peña, E. V., & Kocur, J. (2013). Parents' experiences in the transition of students with autism spectrum disorders to community college. *Journal of Applied Research in the Community College, 20*(2), 29–36.

Popham, W. J. (1999). Why standardized tests don't measure educational quality. *Educational Leadership. 56*(6) 8-15.

Rudestam, K. E., & Newton, R. R. (2007). *Surviving your dissertation: A comprehensive guide to content and process* (3rd ed.). SAGE.

Von Stumm, S., & Plomin, R. (2015). Socioeconomic status and the growth of intelligence from infancy through adolescence. *Intelligence, 48*(7), 30–36. doi:10.1016/j.intell.2014.10.002

Wehman, P., Schall, C., Carr, S., Targett, P., West, M., & Cifu, G. (2014). Transition from school to adulthood for youth with autism spectrum disorder: What we know what we need to know. *Journal of Disability Policy Studies, 25*(1), 30–40. https://doi.org/10.1177/1044207313518071

Wei, X., Wagner, M., Hudson, L., Yu, J. W., & Javitz, H. (2016). The effects of transition planning participation and goal-setting on college enrollment among youth with autism spectrum disorder. *Remedial and Special Education, 37*(1), 3–14. https://doi.org/10.1177/0741932515581495

White, S. W., Ollendick, T. H., & Bray, B. C. (2011). College students on the autism spectrum: Prevalence and associated problems. *Autism, 15*(6), 683–701. https://doi.org/10.1177/1362361310393363

Yin, R. K. (2014). *Case study research: Design and methods* (5th ed.). SAGE.

Individual Scholarly Works Template

Title of the scholarly work:
Is this a journal article, book, or other?
Is it peer-reviewed?
What is(are) the major topic(s) presented?
Which words are repeated often?
How does this scholarly work answer the problem or address the topic?
How does this scholarly work neglect to answer the problem or address the topic?
What evidence does the scholarly work present regarding the problem or topic?
What data collection methods were used?
What data analysis methods were used?
What are the strengths of the scholarly work?
What are the limitations of the scholarly work?
What is the theoretical or conceptual framework, if presented?
Does this relate to your study? If so, how?
What are the results of the study?
Include quotes from the scholarly work below (include the page numbers). Use quotes sparingly.
Include the correctly formatted reference here.
Paste the link to the article here.

Comparative Scholarly Works Template

Title of the first journal article:	
Title of the second journal article:	
What do these articles have in common?	
How are the results of these two articles different?	
How does this information relate to your proposed study?	
Paste the reference and link to the first article here.	
Paste the reference and link to the second article here.	

Action Item Table

Date	Action Item

Appendix D
Educational Report Checklist

Checklist for the Cover Page

- ☐ Does the cover page include a *Title* that is derived from the research question?
- ☐ Does the cover page include *Prepared for* information, including the site name and address?
- ☐ Does the cover page include the *Presented by* information, including the full name of the researcher?
- ☐ Does the cover page include the *Date* the report was completed or presented?

Checklist for a Table of Contents

Does the Table of Contents include the following headings in this order?

- ☐ Executive Summary
- ☐ About the Investigator
- ☐ Permission to Conduct Research
- ☐ Introduction
- ☐ Literature Review
- ☐ Procedures
- ☐ Findings
- ☐ Recommendations
- ☐ References
- ☐ Appendix

Checklist for the Executive Summary

- ☐ Does the Executive Summary include the problem of the study?
- ☐ Does the Executive Summary include the purpose of the research?
- ☐ Does the Executive Summary include the setting?
- ☐ Does the Executive Summary include the rationale for the study?
- ☐ Does the Executive Summary include the central research question?
- ☐ Does the Executive Summary include the procedures?
- ☐ Does the Executive Summary include the recommendations?
- ☐ The Executive Summary is approximately one page (no longer).
- ☐ The Executive Summary does not include quotes.
- ☐ The Executive Summary is in paragraph format.
- ☐ The Executive Summary is written in past tense.

Checklist for About the Investigator

- ☐ Does the About the Investigator section include the researcher's name?

- ☐ Does the About the Investigator section include the researcher's professional credentials?
- ☐ Does the About the Investigator section include a clear description of the researcher's relationship to the educational site?
- ☐ Does the About the Investigator section include biases?
- ☐ Does the About the Investigator section include a professional headshot portrait?
- ☐ The About the Investigator section is written in paragraph format.
- ☐ The About the Investigator section is written in present and/or past tense.
- ☐ The About the Investigator section is less than one page in length.

Checklist for Permission to Conduct the Research

- ☐ Does the Permission to Conduct research section include the name of the gatekeeper(s) and their position (principal, superintendent, etc.)?
- ☐ Does the Permission to Conduct research section include a reference to the appendix where the written permission letter is located? (For example: See Appendix A).
- ☐ The Permission to Conduct the Research section is written in narrative paragraph format.
- ☐ The Permission to Conduct the Research section is written in past tense.

Checklist for Ethical Considerations

- ☐ Does the Ethical Considerations section include a description of ethical treatment of participants specific to your study?
- ☐ Does the Ethical Considerations section include solicitation of participants procedures?
- ☐ Does the Ethical Considerations section include a brief description of the specific participants (teachers, administrators, etc.)?
- ☐ Does the Ethical Considerations section include data protection strategies (i.e., pseudonyms)?
- ☐ Does the Ethical Considerations section include storage of data strategies?
- ☐ Does the Ethical Considerations section include IRB permission, if applicable?
- ☐ The Ethical Considerations section is written in paragraph format.
- ☐ The Ethical Considerations section is written in past tense.

Checklist for an Overview

- ☐ Does the Overview include the purpose of the research?
- ☐ Does the Overview introduce the major headings of the section?

Checklist for the Organizational Profile

- ☐ Does the Organizational Profile include the educational site?
- ☐ Does the Organizational Profile include whether the organization is public or private?
- ☐ Does the Organizational Profile include the geographic location?
- ☐ Does the Organizational Profile include the mission statement?
- ☐ Does the Organizational Profile include demographic information?
- ☐ Does the Organizational Profile include a description of the faculty and/or staff?
- ☐ Does the Organizational Profile include a description of programs and services, if applicable?
- ☐ The Organizational Profile is written in paragraph format.
- ☐ The Organizational Profile is written in past tense.

Checklist for Introduction to the Problem

☐ Does the Introduction to the Problem begin with the problem statement?
☐ Does the Introduction to the Problem include supporting evidence (statistics, facts)?
☐ Does the Introduction to the Problem include what was done in the past to solve the problem?
☐ Does the Introduction to the Problem include what is currently being done to solve the problem?
☐ The Introduction is written in paragraph format.
☐ The Introduction to the Problem is written in past tense.

Checklist for Significance of the Problem

☐ Does the Significance of the Problem include a description of the practical contributions the project makes to the stakeholders and organization?
☐ Does the Significance of the Problem include how the research could improve educational conditions for the community at large?
☐ Does the Significance of the Problem include citations to support assertions?
☐ The Significance of the Problem is written in paragraph format.
☐ The Significance of the Problem is written in past tense.

Checklist for Purpose Statement

☐ Does the Purpose Statement section follow the template for the purpose statement?
☐ Does the Purpose Statement section include the data collection approaches?
☐ Does the Purpose Statement section include details related to each approach (participants, documents, artifacts, etc.)?
☐ The Purpose Statement is written in paragraph format.
☐ The Purpose Statement is written in past tense.

Checklist for the Central Research Question

☐ Is the Central Research Question derived from the problem and purpose statements?
☐ Does the Central Research Question follow one of the two formats provided in the Central Research Question section of this textbook?

Checklist for the Definitions

☐ Do the Definitions include all terms relevant to the study?
☐ Are the Definitions defined using the literature and not a dictionary?
☐ Are the Definitions cited?
☐ Are Definitions presented in list format?

Checklist for the Literature Review

☐ The Literature Review begins with an Overview.
☐ The Overview is followed by the Narrative Review.
☐ The Narrative Review presents justification for the rationale for the study.
☐ The Literature Review is not presented as a collection of citations from multiple journal articles.
☐ The Literature Review is presented as a synthesis of the literature.

☐ The Literature Review demonstrates a clear connection between prior research and the proposed research.

☐ The historical context of the problem of practice is clearly presented.

☐ A critical analysis of the literature is evident.

☐ The cause of the problem, as identified in the literature, is presented (if known).

☐ Prior solutions are presented.

☐ Solutions to the problem found in the literature are presented.

☐ Most journal articles (approximately 80%) are less than five years since publication.

☐ The Literature Review is focused on solving the problem.

☐ The authors' voice is heard throughout the literature review.

☐ Each paragraph begins with a topic sentence.

☐ The Literature Review is written concisely.

Checklist for the Interview Procedures

☐ Does the Interview Procedures include the type of interview (structures, unstructured, semi-structured) and its justification (including a citation)?

☐ Does the Interview Procedures include sampling type (purposeful sampling, snowball, etc.)?

☐ Does the Interview Procedures identify the participants?

☐ Does the Interview Procedures identify the rationale for participant selection?

☐ Does the Interview Procedures include how the interviews were conducted (face-to-face, phone, etc.)?

☐ Does the Interview Procedures briefly explain data analysis procedures?

☐ Does the Interview Procedures include the number of interview questions?

☐ Does the Interview Procedures include the interview questions and their rationale (the majority of questions should be cited using the literature)?

☐ The Interview Procedures is written in paragraph format.

☐ The Interview Procedures is written in past tense.

Checklist for the Interview Findings

☐ Does the Interview Findings include the type of interview?

☐ Does the Interview Findings include a brief overview of the procedures?

☐ Does the Interview Findings include a Description of Participants?

☐ Does the Interview Findings include Interview Results in the form of tables to include coding, quotations, and frequency word counts?

☐ Does the Interview Findings include a discussion of the findings and interpretation?

☐ Does the Interview Findings include a discussion of themes with supporting evidence?

☐ The Interview Findings is written in paragraph format.

☐ The Interview Findings is written in past tense.

Checklist for the Survey Procedures

☐ Does the Survey Procedures include the type of survey (Likert scale, multiple choice, true/false, etc.) and its justification?

☐ Does the Survey Procedures include sampling type (purposeful sampling, snowball, etc.)?

☐ Does the Survey Procedures identify the participants?

☐ Does the Survey Procedures identify the rationale for participant selection?

☐ Does the Survey Procedures include how the survey was conducted?

☐ Does the Survey Procedures briefly explain data analysis procedures?

☐ Does the Survey Procedures include number of survey questions?

☐ Does the Survey Procedures include the survey questions and their rationale (the majority of questions should be cited using the literature)?

☐ The Survey Procedures is written in paragraph format.

☐ The Survey Procedures is written in past tense.

Checklist for the Survey Findings

☐ Does the Survey Findings include the type of scale?

☐ Does the Survey Findings include a brief overview of the procedures?

☐ Does the Survey Findings include a Description of Participants?

☐ Does the Survey Findings include Survey Results in the form of tables?

☐ Does the Survey Findings include a discussion of the findings and interpretation?

☐ Does the Survey Findings include a discussion of themes with supporting evidence?

☐ The Survey Findings is written in paragraph format.

☐ The Survey Findings is written in past tense.

Checklist for the Documents Procedures

☐ Does the Documents Procedures section include the type of document?

☐ Does the Documents Procedures section identify the rationale for using the documents?

☐ Does the Documents Procedures section include how the documents were obtained?

☐ Does the Documents Procedures section briefly explain how data were analyzed?

☐ The Documents Procedures section is written in paragraph format.

☐ The Documents Procedures section is written in past tense.

Checklist for the Documents Findings

☐ Does the Document Findings section include the type of documents analyzed?

☐ Does the Document Findings section include a brief overview of the procedures?

☐ Does the Document Findings section include results in the form of tables and figures?

☐ Does the Document Findings section include an interpretation of the data?

☐ Does the Document Findings section include a discussion of themes with supporting evidence?

☐ The Document Findings section is written in paragraph format.

☐ The Document Findings section is written in past tense.

Checklist for the Recommendations

☐ Does the Recommendations section include the Purpose of the study?

☐ Does the Recommendations section include the Central Research question?

☐ Does the Recommendations section list specific recommendations numerically?

☐ Does the Recommendations section discuss each recommendation separately using headings?

☐ Does the Recommendations section include justification for each recommendation based on the literature review and data collected?

☐ Does the Recommendations section include the implications (pros and cons)?

Checklist for the Roles and Responsibilities

☐ Does the Roles and Responsibilities section include each recommendation under its own heading?

☐ Does the Roles and Responsibilities section describe the roles and responsibilities of each person needed to accomplish the recommendation?

☐ Does the Roles and Responsibilities section include possible personnel implications (hiring, training, certifications)?

☐ Does the Roles and Responsibilities section describe specific responsibilities assigned to each role?

Checklist for the Resources Needed

☐ Does the Resources section include a heading for each of the recommendations?

☐ Does the Resources section include enough detail to account for all resources?

☐ Does the Resources section include numerical values, if applicable?

Checklist for the Timeline

☐ Does the Timeline include a timeline for each recommendation in table format?

☐ Does the Timeline include the date and action for completing each item?

☐ Does the Timeline include enough detail that the recommendation could be implemented effectively?

Checklist for the Summary

☐ Does the Summary include the goal of the study?

☐ Does the Summary include the data collection methods used?

☐ Does the Summary include one or two take-aways from the Implications section?

☐ Does the Summary include the recommendations to solve the problem or improve the practice?

Index